STUDIOS

TALMA

From the same author:
– *Geopolitics of Cryptocurrencies* (with Nancy Gomez) ;
– *L'Arme climatique - La manipulation du climat par les miltaires* ;
– *The Mystery of the Ancient Maps.*

To be published:
– *L'Arme environnementale.*

Original title: *Le FBI, complice du 11 Septembre*

Talma Studios International Ltd.
Pod 2, The Old Station House
15A Main St – Blackrock
Co Dublin A94 T8P8
Ireland
www.talmastudios.com
info@talmastudios.com

ISBN: 978-1-913191-00-9

Patrick Pasin

THE FBI, ACCOMPLICE OF 9/11

Translated from French

In memory of all victims of 9/11 and wars that followed.

Accomplice: partner in crime.

The Oxford Thesaurus

Introduction

Like you probably do, I remember what I was doing on September 11, 2001, when I heard what had just happened in New York. It was little over 3 pm in Paris when I hastily left my office to follow the events as they unfolded on television.

The news seemed contradictory and confusing, especially in Washington, but this was all but normal in such a distressing situation. What did surprise me was the lack of images showing the aftermath at the Pentagon, a plume of smoke from afar being the only hint. Yet there are cameras all over D.C. and the omnipresent media are constantly in search of the next big scoop. These thoughts quickly evaporated, because I was already sure of one thing: what happened on 9/11 would forever change the world.

These events then came knocking on my door as publisher: Thierry Meyssan and his team published some photos of the Pentagon's facade on their website, L'Asile Utopique. They added a scale representation of the Boeing 757-200 corresponding to American Airlines flight 77. It seems nearly impossible that a forty-meter wide plane could have hit the building and then disappeared into a hole but five to six meters wide.

I suggested to Thierry Meyssan that we have dinner together and discuss the idea of a book on his research. During the four-hour conversation, I played devil's advocate and he systematically presented arguments based on multiple sources, both official and media.

We immediately agreed on contractual conditions and three months later, at the end of February 2002, he handed me the commissioned manuscript. All that remained was to carry out the various editorial steps preceding the publishing. I suggested *L'Effroyable Imposture*[1] as title, with the catchphrase "No plane crashed into the Pentagon!"

---

1. The title in English is *9/11 The Big Lie*, Thierry Meyssan, Carnot, 2002.

Government Reactions

Worldwide success came quickly with translations into nearly thirty languages, not to mention all the pirate versions.

One of the first official reactions from the United States came from the FBI, which gave the following statement on April 2, 2002:

> To even suggest that AA77 did not crash into the Pentagon on September 11 is the ultimate insult to the memory of 59 men, women and children on AA77 and the 125 dedicated military and civilian workers in the Pentagon who were ruthlessly murdered by terrorists on September 11.[2]

A few days later, a similar statement was made by Victoria Clarke on behalf of the Department of Defense:

> I think even the suggestion of it is ludicrous. And finally, it is just an incredible insult to the friends and the relatives and the family members of the almost 200 people that got killed here on September 11th and the thousands who were killed in New York.[3]

The book was first published in French, then in English. Naturally, there were multiple attempts to hinder the spreading of Meyssan's work. For example, a few weeks before the release of *9/11 The Big Lie*, *U.S. News and World Report* published an article denouncing Amazon for being about to sell an anti-American book on September 11. I wrote to Jeff Bezos, founder and CEO, to explain that there was nothing anti-American in the book because, in memory of the victims, everything had to be done to identify and punish the perpetrators, no matter their identity. I did not know whether the letter had any effect, or even if he received it. Regardless, the book went on sale on Amazon in the United States.

---

2. *The New Pearl Harbor*, David Ray Griffin, Arris Books, p. 46.
3. *The New Pearl Harbor*, David Ray Griffin, p. 46.

In March 2002, Thierry Meyssan showed me new pictures and testimonies of the Pentagon attack that corroborated his work. I suggested writing a second book focused solely on Washington, because the information he discovered debunked the government version. Its title came as no surprise: *The Pentagate*. It weakened the certainties of the still numerous believers of the government narrative. An English television presenter, who had read both books, told him that she had no counter-arguments. The only reason she chose to believe the version implicating bin Laden was because it helped her sleep at night. However, many rather take refuge in the stance: "Yes, but it is conspiracy theory."

They are right, because 9/11 can be summed up as a conspiracy theory with two versions:

– the government version of the conspiracy: fanatical Islamists attacked America through a highly elaborate military operation, directed from... a cave in Afghanistan by Osama bin Laden;

– ours: from the analysis of facts and the multiple anomalies that have been piling up, we can only deduce that the government version is a lie. In time, it is becoming increasingly clear that culprits should be fished out from what is called "the Deep State." Who else could have organized and perpetrated such an atrocity? There must have been external complicities, of course.

We are often told that such a conspiracy would have required thousands of accomplices within the inner circle, which seems impossible without any leaks. But here, a few dozen individuals at most, placed in key positions, could have been enough.

So that is where the FBI, or Federal Bureau of Investigation, comes in. Indeed, since the very beginning of the investigation its actions have been surprising, if not contradictory. It is what this book seeks to study based on official statements and documents. This includes *The 9/11 Commission Report*[4], by the Kean-Hamilton Commission, created by Congress and the President under the name *National*

---

4. *The 9/11 Commission Report,* authorized edition, W. W. Norton & Company.

Commission on Terrorists Attacks Upon the United States[5] (Public Law 107-306, November 27, 2002)—as well as other official sources and mainstream media.

Researchers who have picked up on the inconsistencies in the government version will also play a major role, namely Thierry Meyssan, Paul Thompson, David Ray Griffin, Peter Lance, Nafeez Ahmed, Michel Chossudovsky, Webster Griffin Tarpley, Craig Unger... They went further and have generally studied in more detail most of the points covered in this book. The *modus operandi* here is not to highlight what has already been analyzed so much as provide a summary of actions committed by those who could be seen as responsible—if not directly, then at least by complicity through inaction. Ultimately, it was incredible to see the lack of accountability throughout this event that took so many lives and continues to poison the world. Some of the guilty, as defined above, even received promotions afterwards.

For national security organizations that were already consuming a sizeable portion of the nation's resources at the time, explaining 9/11 through "failures," "poor organization," "we could not imagine," and similar watered-down statements seems more like an alibi hiding what appears to be blatant sabotage and complicity at the highest levels. It is also a direct insult to the memory of all innocent victims of the tragedy for whom justice is sought.

Since its duty is to enforce the law and leading the investigation on 9/11, the FBI will be the focus in this short and non-exhaustive study.[6] This, to bring to light actions carried out before, during and after the events that will mark Humanity for a long time.

This study's goal will not be to *accuse*, but *question* the accountability of the involved parties and actions surrounding one of the most shocking events in recent history.

---

5. Generally, it is referred to here as "the Commission."
6. Despite the thousands of pages read and dozens of documentaries watched on the matter, it is possible that some updates or complementary information have not been included. It is, indeed, impossible to be exhaustive on the subject of 9/11.

Context
The FBI and Terrorism

"The Justice Department and the FBI
At the federal level, much law enforcement activity is concentrated in the Department of Justice. For countering terrorism, the dominant agency under Justice is the Federal Bureau of Investigation. The FBI does not have a general grant of authority but instead works under specific statutory authorizations. Most of its work is done in local offices called field offices. There are 56 of them, each covering a specified geographic area, and each quite separate from all others. Prior to 9/11, the special agent in charge was in general free to set his or her office's priorities and assign personnel accordingly.

The office's priorities were driven by two primary concerns. First, performance in the Bureau was generally measured against statistics such as numbers of arrests, indictments, prosecutions, and convictions. Counterterrorism and counterintelligence work, often involving lengthy intelligence investigations that might never have positive or quantifiable results, was not career-enhancing."[7]

Should we believe that the American people was not protected from 9/11 attacks due to career aspirations?
The *Report* stated the following:

> Most agents who reached management ranks had little counterterrorism experience. Second, priorities were driven at the local level by the field offices, whose concerns centered on traditional crimes such as white-collar offenses and those pertaining to drugs and gangs. Individual field offices made choices to serve local priorities, not national priorities.

---

7. *The 9/11 Commission Report*, pp. 74-75.

We will see that this was not the case at all, and in writing this the Commission was almost committing an offense against what we could call "basic agents" who did more than their duty in various cases (see next chapter). Had they been listened to, 9/11 would never have happened:

> The Bureau also operates under an "office of origin" system. To avoid duplication and possible conflicts, the FBI designates a single office to be in charge of an entire investigation. Because the New York Field Office indicted Bin Ladin prior to the East Africa bombings, it became the office of origin for all Bin Ladin cases, including the east Africa bombings and later the attack on the USS *Cole*[8]. Most of the FBI's institutional knowledge on Bin Ladin resided there. [...]
> In 1986, Congress authorized the FBI to investigate terrorist attacks against Americans that occur outside the United States. Three years later, it added authority for the FBI to make arrests abroad without consent from the host country. Meanwhile, a task force headed by Vice President George H. W. Bush had endorsed a concept already urged by Director of Central Intelligence William Casey—a Counterterrorist Center, where the FBI, the CIA, and other organizations could work together on international terrorism. While it was distinctly a CIA entity, the FBI detailed officials to work at the Center and obtained leads that helped in the capture of persons wanted for trial in the United States.

It will later be shown that this point is of paramount importance. As the *Commission Report* puts it,

---

8. "On 12 October 2000, *Cole* was the target of an attack carried out by al-Qaeda in the Yemeni port of Aden, when two suicide bombersdetonated explosives carried in a small boat near the warship, killing 17 sailors, injuring 39 others, and damaging the ship." https://en.wikipedia.org/wiki/USS_Cole_(DDG-67)

the strengths that the FBI brought to counterterrorism were nowhere more brilliantly on display than in the case of Pan American Flight 103, bound from London to New York, which blew up over Lockerbie, Scotland, in December 1988, killing 270 people.

Then the conclusion of the paragraph on Pan Am 103 says that

it also showed again how—given a case to solve—the FBI remained capable of extraordinary investigative success.

How could we doubt that?

Terrorism and Priorities

Chosen by President Clinton in 1993, Louis Freeh became the Director of the Bureau until June 2001. According to the *Report* (p. 76),

he "recognized terrorism as a major threat, […]" but his "efforts did not, however, translate into a significant shift of resources to counterterrorism."

It was only in 1998 that things changed:

For the first time, the FBI designated national and economic security, including counterterrorism, as its top priority. Dale Watson, who would later become the head of the new Counterterrorism Division, said that after the East Africa bombings, 'the light came on' that cultural change had to occur within the FBI.

The stakes were high, because

if successfully implemented, [the measures] would have been a major step toward addressing terrorism systematically, rather than as individual unrelated cases. But the plan did not succeed. Again and again.

A Known Threat—The Millennium Plot

As January 1st, 2000, drew near, authorities learned from the Jordanian government of an al-Qaeda millennium bombing plot with several attacks planned on America. Richard Clarke, the "tsar" of counterterrorism, was informed and he implemented a plan to neutralize the threat.[9] The plan, approved by President Clinton, focused on harassing and disrupting al-Qaeda members throughout the world with the help of all U.S. embassies, military bases, police departments, other agencies, etc.

> The FBI is put on heightened alert, counterterrorism teams are dispatched overseas, a formal ultimatum is given to the Taliban to keep al-Qaeda under control, and friendly intelligence agencies are asked to help. There are Cabinet-level meetings nearly every day dealing with terrorism. (*Washington Post*, 4/20/00; Associated Press, 6/28/02).[10]

This led to the arrest of Ahmed Ressam by border patrol agent Diana Dean on December 14, 1999, in Port Angeles, Washington, with more than 50 kg of bomb-making chemicals and detonator components found inside his rental car. He subsequently admitted that he had planned to carry out an attack on Los Angeles airport. As the *New York Times* reported,

---

9. *Against All Enemies*, Richard Clarke, 3/04, pp. 205, 211, quoted in *The Terror Timeline*, p. 79.
10. *The Terror Timeline*, p. 79.

The arrest of Ahmed Ressam was the clearest sign that Osama bin Laden was trying to bring the jihad to the United States. […] "That was a wake-up call," a senior law enforcement officer said […]. Just as the embassy bombings had exposed the threat of Al Qaeda overseas, the millennium plot revealed gaping vulnerabilities at home.

"If you understood Al Qaeda, you knew something was going to happen," said Robert M. Bryant, who was the deputy director of the F.B.I. when he retired in 1999. "You knew they were going to hit us, but you didn't know where. It just made me sick on Sept. 11. I cried when those towers came down."[11]

Despite this arrest that thwarted several other bombings and identified a string of accomplices in New York, Boston and Seattle, "Clarke claimed the FBI generally remains unhelpful." (*Newsweek*, 3/31/04).[12] He later said:

"I think a lot of the FBI leadership for the first time realized that...there probably were al-Qaeda people in the United States. They realized that only after they looked at the results of the investigation of the millennium bombing plot." (PBS Frontline, 10/3/02). Yet Clinton's National Security Adviser Sandy Berger says, "Until the very end of our time in office, the view we received from the [FBI] was that al-Qaeda had limited capacity to operate in the U.S. and any presence here was under surveillance." No analysis is done before 9/11 to investigate just how big that presence might be. (*Washington Post*, 9/20/02).[13]

---

11. *Planning for Terror but Failing to Act*, Judith Miller, Jeff Gerth, Don Van Natta Jr., *The New York Times*, December 30, 2001.
12. *The Terror Timeline*, p. 80.
13. *The Terror Timeline*, p. 80.

In December 1999, the CIA confirmed the threat:

> Because the U.S. is [bin Laden]'s ultimate goal...we must assume that several of these targets will be in the U.S. (9/11 Congressional Inquiry, 7/24/03; *Time*, 8/4/02). Since late 1999, there has been intelligence that targets in Washington and New York would be attacked at this time. (9/11 Congressional Inquiry, 9/18/02).[14]

Who can still talk, at the FBI and elsewhere, about the surprise element surrounding the al-Qaeda attacks that would occur less than two years later? Why were appropriate measures not implemented when there was still time and the threat was taking shape on national territory?

A Known Threat—A Murderous Attack

It sounds strange to hear Dale Watson, who would later be named Executive Assistant Director for Counterterrorism/Counter-intelligence, say that "the light came on" after the East Africa bombings of 1998. Especially since one had occurred in **the USA** itself five years earlier. On February 26, 1993, the World Trade Center (WTC) was bombed, leaving six people dead, more than a thousand wounded and cost more than $500 million in damages.
The *Report* read:

> an FBI agent at the scene described the relatively low number of fatalities as a miracle. [...]
> The New York Field Office of the FBI took control of the local investigation and, in the end, set a pattern for future management of terrorist incidents.

---

14. *The Terror Timeline*, p. 80.

Four features of this episode have significance for the story of 9/11.

First, the bombing signaled a new terrorist challenge, one whose rage and malice had no limit. Ramzi Yousef, the Sunni extremist who planted the bomb, said later that he had hoped to kill 250,000 people. (pp. 71-72)

Yousef was finally captured in Pakistan following the discovery of the Manila air plot by the Filipino police in January 1995. It was an elaborate plan to place bombs on board a dozen trans-Pacific airliners and set them off simultaneously.

In other words, the FBI knew that terrorists wanted to kill at least 250,000 people using airliners, and its directors were unable to take preventive action? Could it be that they did not surveil these extremist networks in NYC mosques, despite several warnings including the World Trade Center bombing and the attack on the USS *Cole* in October 2000?

Would it be reasonable to believe that they had not received any intelligence? Is it credible that the FBI knew absolutely nothing of 9/11? Is it sure that the FBI could not have prevented it?

Chapter 9/2

The FBI Knew

Robert Swan Mueller III (born August 7, 1944) served as the sixth Director of the Federal Bureau of Investigation from 2001 to 2013, appointed by President Bush one week before 9/11. On September 14, he declared:

> There were no warning signs that I'm aware of that would indicate this type of operation in the country.[15]

He had barely arrived, it is understandable that he had not previously received any information on the threat. His statement is confirmed in the Joint Inquiry's final report summary conducted by the House and Senate intelligence committees:

> While the Intelligence Community had amassed a great deal of valuable intelligence regarding Osama bin Ladin and his terrorist activities, none of it identified the time, place, and specific nature of the attacks that were planned for September 11, 2001.[16]

However, FBI agents repeatedly accused their headquarters of blocking investigations before 9/11 that could have prevented the attacks. Thus, the list of information showing that the FBI knew what was going to happen, including the day and targets, is highly disturbing. Nevertheless, authorities never stopped claiming the opposite throughout the following years. What is even more disconcerting are the choices made regularly at the expense of the American people's security, as will be shown.

---

15. *The New Pearl Harbor*, p. 69.
16. *The New Pearl Harbor*, p. 69.

More than Ten Years of Terror

Let us start with extracts from *The Terror Timeline*[17], a remarkable piece of work put together by Paul Thompson and the Center for Cooperative Research:

> July 1990: Blind Sheikh on Terrorist Watch List Enters U.S.
> Despite being on a U.S. terrorist watch list for three years, radical Muslim leader Sheikh Omar Abdul-Rahman, dubbed the "Blind Sheikh," enters the U.S. on a "much-disputed" tourist issued by an undercover CIA agent. (*Village Voice*, 3/30/93; *Atlantic Monthly*, 5/96; *1000 Years for Revenge*, by Peter Lance, 9/03, p. 42). Heavily involved with the CIA and Pakistani ISI efforts to defeat the Soviets in Afghanistan, [...] yet he never hid his prime goals to overthrow the governments of Egypt and the U.S. (*Atlantic Monthly*, 5/96), where he immediately begins setting up a terrorist network in the U.S. (*Village Voice*, 3/30/93). [...] Egyptian intelligence warns the U.S. that he is planning new terrorist attacks, and on November 12, 1992, terrorists connected to him machine-gun a busload of Western tourists in Egypt. Still, he will continue to live freely in New York City (*Village Voice*, 3/30/93), but he will finally be arrested in 1993 and convinced of assisting in the 1993 WTC bombing. (*Atlantic Monthly*, 5/96).[18]
>
> November 5, 1990: First bin Laden-Related
> Terror Attack on U.S.
> Egyptian-American El Sayyid Nosair assassinates controversial right-wing Zionist leader Rabbi Meir Kahane, whose organization, the Jewish Defense League, was linked to

17. The information in this paragraph stems mainly from *The Terror Timeline, Day By Day, Minute By Minute: A Comprehensive Chronicle of the Road to 9/11-and America's Response*, Paul Thompson and the Center for Cooperative Research, ReganBooks, 2004. HistoryCommons.org also provides an exceptional chronology.
18. *The Terror Timeline*, p. 8.

dozens of bombings and is ranked by the FBI as the most lethal domestic terrorist group in the U.S. at the time. […] (*Village Voice*, 3/30/93). […] Nosair is captured and files found in his possession give details of a terrorist cell, mention al-Qaeda, and discuss the destruction of tall U.S. buildings. Incredibly, this vital information is not translated until years later. (ABC News, 8/16/02). […] Bin Laden contributes to Nosair's defense fund. Many of those involved in Kahane's assassination will plan the 1993 WTC bombing. As one FBI agent puts it, "The fact is that in 1990, myself and my detectives, we had in our office in handcuffs, the people who blew up the World Trade Center in '93. We were told to release them." (ABC News, 8/16/02).[19]

Knowing that these individuals were involved in an assassination, who could have given such an order and for what purpose? Were they protected and by whom?

September 1, 1992: U.S. Misses Opportunity to Stop First WTC Bombing and Discover al-Qaeda

Terrorists Ahmad Ajaj and Ramzi Yousef enter the U.S. together. Ajaj is arrested at Kennedy Airport in New York City. Yousef is not arrested, and later, he masterminds the 1993 bombing of the WTC. "The U.S. government was pretty sure Ajaj was a terrorist from the moment he stepped foot on U.S. soil," because his "suitcases were stuffed with fake passports, fake IDs and a cheat sheet on how to lie to U.S. immigration inspectors," plus "two handwritten notebooks filled with bomb recipes, six bomb-making manuals, four how-to videotapes concerning weaponry, and an advanced guide to surveillance training." However, Ajaj is charged only with passport fraud, and serves a six-month sentence. From prison, Ajaj frequently

19. *The Terror Timeline*, p. 8-9.

calls Yousef and others in the 1993 WTC bombing plot, but no one translates the calls until long after the bombing. (*Los Angeles Times*, 10/14/01). [...][20]

Not only did nobody translate the calls, but how could those he called not have been put under surveillance when his terrorist intent was clear? Is this not the foundation of intelligence and the role of the FBI?

1993-1998: Al-Qaeda Double Agent Is Arrested and Then Released; Tells Secrets About al-Qaeda

Canadian police arrest Ali Mohamed, a high-ranking al-Qaeda figure. However, they release him when the FBI says he is a U.S. agent. (*Globe and Mail,* 11/22/01). Mohamed, a former U.S. Army sergeant, will continue to work for al-Qaeda for a number of years. He trains bin Laden's personal bodyguards and trains a terrorist cell in Kenya that later blows up the U.S. embassy there. Meanwhile, between 1993 and 1997 he tells secrets to the FBI about al-Qaeda's operations. He is re-arrested in late 1998 and subsequently convicted for his role in the 1998 U.S. embassy bombing in Kenya. (CNN, 10/30/98; *Independent*, 11/1/98). [...][21]

February 26, 1993: WTC Is Bombed but Does Not Collapsed, as Hoped

An attempt to topple the WTC fails, but six people are killed in the misfired blast. Analysts later determine that had the terrorists not made a minor error in the placement of the bomb, both towers could have fallen and up to 50,000 people could have been killed. Ramzi Yousef, who has close ties to bin Laden, organizes the attempt. (Congressional Hearings,

---

20. *The Terror Timeline*, p. 9.
21. *The Terror Timeline*, p. 10.

2/24/98). [...] One of the attackers even left a message found by investigators stating, "Next time, it will be very precise."[22]

Aware of the WTC Bomb Plot?

An article from the *New York Times* published on October 28, 1993, began as follows[23]:

> Law-enforcement officials were told that terrorists were building a bomb that was eventually used to blow up the World Trade Center, and they planned to thwart the plotters by secretly substituting harmless powder for the explosives, an informer said after the blast.
>
> The informer was to have helped the plotters build the bomb and supply the fake powder, but the plan was called off by an F.B.I. supervisor who had other ideas about how the informer, Emad A. Salem, should be used, the informer said.
>
> The account, which is given in the transcript of hundreds of hours of tape recordings Mr. Salem secretly made of his talks with law-enforcement agents, portrays the authorities as in a far better position than previously known to foil the Feb. 26 bombing of New York City's tallest towers.

A correction is published the next day:

> An article yesterday about accounts of a plot to build a bomb that was eventually exploded at the World Trade Center referred imprecisely in some copies to what Federal officials knew about the plan before the blast. Transcripts of tapes made secretly by an informant, Emad A. Salem, quote him as saying he warned the Government that a bomb was being

---

22. *The Terror Timeline*, p. 11.
23. *Tapes Depict Proposal to Thwart Bomb Used in Trade Center Blast*, Ralph Blumental, *New York Times*, October 28, 1993.

built. But the transcripts do not make clear the extent to which the Federal authorities knew that the target was the World Trade Center.

The article does not allow to conclude that the FBI had been aware of an imminent attack on the WTC, nor that it could have prevented the bombing. But, at the very least, it confirmed the existence of a terrorist cell in New York, one that intended to set off explosives, and that an infiltration operation had been successful. In fact, the role that the FBI played to prevent this operation that left six dead and more than a thousand wounded—or let it happen—was never clarified.

More than Ten Years of Terror, continued

Coming back then, to the valuable information in *The Terror Timeline*:

1994-September 2001: Evidence of Terrorist Connections in Arizona Obtained by Local Agents Repeatedly Ignored by FBI Headquarters

By 1990, Arizona became one of the main centers in the U.S. for radical Muslims, and it remained so throughout this period. However, terrorism remained a low priority for the Phoenix, Arizona, FBI office. Around 1990, hijacker Hani Hanjour moved to Arizona for the first time and he spent much of the next decade in the state. The FBI apparently remained oblivious of Hanjour, though one FBI informant claimed that, by 1998, they "knew everything about the guy." (*New York Times*, 6/19/02). In 1994, the Phoenix FBI office uncovered startling evidence connecting Arizona to radical Muslim terrorists. The office videotapes two men trying to recruit a Phoenix FBI informant to be a suicide bomber. One of the men was linked to terrorist leader Sheikh Omar Abdul-Rahman (*Los Angeles Times*, 5/26/02; *New York Times*, 6/19/02).[24]

There is more about the Arizona terrorist cell:

In 1998, the office's international terrorism squad investigates, as best they could, a Middle Eastern extremist taking flight lessons at a Phoenix airport. FBI agent Ken Williams initiates an investigation into the possibility of terrorists learning to fly aircraft, but he has no easy way to query a central FBI database about similar cases. Because of this and other FBI communication problems, he remains unaware of most U.S. intelligence reports about the potential use of airplanes as weapons, as well as other specific FBI warnings issued in 1998 and 1999 concerning terrorists training at U.S. flight schools. (9/11 Congressional Inquiry, 7/24/03).[25] (we come back to the "Phoenix Memo" in the following chapter.)

1994: Al-Qaeda-connected Group Tries to Fly Airplane into Eiffel Tower; Similar Attempts Elsewhere

[...] *Time* magazine details the Eiffel Tower suicide plan in a cover story. (*Time*, 1/9/05; *1000 Years for Revenge*, by Peter Lance, 9/03, p. 258).[26]

December 12, 1994: Operation Bojinka Trial Run Fails, but Kills One

Terrorist Ramzi Yousef attempts a trial run of Operation Bojinka, planting a small bomb on a Philippine Airlines flight to Tokyo, and disembarking on a stopover before the bomb is detonated. The bomb explodes, killing one man and injuring several others.

---

24. *The Terror Timeline*, p. 11-12.
25. *The Terror Timeline*, p.12.
26. *The Terror Timeline*, p. 12.

It would have successfully caused the plane to crash if not for the heroic efforts of the pilot. (*Los Angeles Times*, 9/1/02; Congressional Inquiry, 9/18/02).[27]

It is impossible to believe that the FBI did not hear about this attack, even more so on a flight to Japan where the Bureau is present and tracking Yakuza trafficking, among other activity.

January 6, 1995: Pope Assassination and Bojinka Plot to Bomb a Dozen Airplanes is Foiled

Responding to an apartment fire, Philippine investigators uncover an al-Qaeda plot to assassinate the Pope that is scheduled to take place when he visits the Philippines one week later. While investigating that scheme, they also uncover Operation Bojinka, planned by the same people: 1993 WTC bomber Ramzi Yousef and 9/11 mastermind Khalid Shaikh Mohammed. (*Independent*, 6/6/02; *Los Angeles Times*, 6/24/02; *Los Angeles Times*, 9/1/02). The first phase of the plan is to explode 11 or 12 passenger planes over the Pacific Ocean. (Agence France-Presse, 12/8/01). Had this plot been successful, up to 4,000 people would have been killed in planes flying to Los Angeles, San Francisco, Honolulu, and New York. (*Insight*, 5/27/02). All the bombs would be planted at about the same time, but some would be timed to go off weeks or even months later. Presumably worldwide air travel could be interrupted for months. (*1000 Years for Revenge*, by Peter Lance, 9/03, pp. 260-261). This phase of Operation Bojinka was scheduled to go forward just two weeks later, on January 21. (*The Cell*, by John Miller, Michael Stone, and Chris Mitchell, 8/02, p. 124; *Insight*, 5/27/02).[28]

---

27. *The Terror Timeline*, p. 12.
28. *The Terror Timeline*, pp. 12-13.

Again, the FBI must have been aware of this plot threatening the United States, which is indeed confirmed below:

> February 1995: Bojinka "Second Wave" Fully Revealed
> to Philippines Investigators; Information Given to U.S.
> As Colonel Mendoza, the Philippines investigator, continues to interrogate Operation Bojinka plotter Abdul Hakim Murad, details of a post-Bojinka "second wave" emerge. Author Peter Lance calls this phase "a virtual blueprint of the 9/11 attacks." Murad reveals a plan to hijack commercial airliners at some point after the effect of Bojinka dies down. Murad himself had been training in the U.S. for this plot. He names the buildings that would be targeted for attack: CIA headquarters, the Pentagon, an unidentified nuclear power plant, the Transamerica Tower in San Francisco, the Sears Tower, and the World Trade Center. Murad continues to reveal more information about this plot until he is handed over to the FBI in April. (*1000 Years for Revenge*, by Peter Lance, 9/03, pp. 278-280). He identifies approximately ten other men who met him at the flight schools or were getting similar training. They came from Sudan, United Arab Emirates, Saudi Arabia, and Pakistan. Apparently, none of these pilots match the names of any of the 9/11 hijackers. However, he also gives information pointing to the terrorist Hambali through a front company named Konsonjaya. Hambali later hosts an important al-Qaeda meeting attended by two of the 9/11 hijackers. (Associated Press, 3/5/02). Colonel Mendoza even makes a flow chart connecting many key players together, including bin Laden, bin Laden's brother-in-law Mohammed Jamal Khalifa, Ramzi Yousef, and 9/11 mastermind Khalid Shaikh Mohammed (named as Salem Ali a.k.a. Mohmad). Philippine authorities later claim that they provide all this information to U.S. authorities, but the U.S. fails to follow up

on any of it. (*1000 Years for Revenge*, by Peter Lance, 9/03, pp. 303-4). Khalifa is in U.S. custody and released even after the Philippine authorities provide this information about him.[29]

Spring 1995: More Evidence That the WTC
Remains a Terrorist Target

In the wake of uncovering the Operation Bojinka plot, Philippine authorities find a letter on a computer disc written by the terrorists who had planned the failed 1993 WTC bombing. This letter apparently was never sent, but its contents are revealed in 1998 congressional testimony. (Congressional Hearings, 2/24/98). The Manila police chief also reports discovering a statement from bin Laden around this time that, although they failed to blow up the WTC in 1993, "on the second attempt they would be successful." (Agence France-Press, 9/13/01).[30]

May 11, 1995: FBI Memo Fails to Mention
Operation Boiinka "Second Wave"

FBI agents, having held Operation Bojinka plotter Abdul Hakim Murad for about a month, write a memo containing what they have learned from interrogating him. The memo contains many interesting revelations, including that Ramzi Yousef, a mastermind of the 1993 World Trade Center bombing, "wanted to return to the United States in the future to bomb the World Trade Center a second time." However, this memo does not contain a word about the second wave of Operation Bojinka to fly about 12 hijacked airplanes into prominent U.S. buildings- even though Murad had recently fully confessed this plot to Philippines investigators, who claim they turned over tapes, transcripts, and reports with Murad's confessions of the plot to the U.S. when they handed over Murad. It has not been

---

29. *The Terror Timeline*, pp. 13-14.
30. *The Terror Timeline*, p. 14.

explained why this plot is not mentioned in the FBI's summary of Murad's interrogation. (*1000 Years for Revenge*, by Peter Lance, 9/03, pp. 280-82). After 9/11, a Philippine investigator will refer to this third plot when he says of the 9/11 attacks, "It's Bojinka. We told the Americans everything about Bojinka. Why didn't they pay attention?" (*Washington Post*, 9/23/01).[31]

This is indeed the question we are entitled to ask. Especially since we are only quoting a few excerpts from *The Terror Timeline*, which offers dozens of pages detailing such alerts, each with growing precision and detail until the September 11 attacks. It is impossible to believe that the attention of authorities in charge of the American people's security had not been attracted. These warnings were numerous, converging, and confirmed by several foreign countries.

Not Only the FBI

Let us momentarily step outside the scope of our FBI-focused study, highlighting some examples of warnings received by the United States from abroad hinting that a major terrorist operation was being prepared on its soil.

– On the CIA's side, in August 2009:

> Former CIA agent Robert Baer reportedly told the CIA's Counter-Terrorism Center that he had learned from a military associate of a Persian Gulf prince that 'a spectacular terrorist operation' was about to take place.[32]

---

31. *The Terror Timeline*, p. 15.
32. Robert Baer, *See No Evil: The True Story of a Ground Soldier in the CIA's War on Terrorism* (New York: Crown Pub, 2002), 270–71; Bill Gertz, *Breakdown: How America's Intelligence Failures Led to September 11* (Washington: Regnery, 2002), 55–58; and *Financial Times*, January 12, 2002; all cited in *September 11: Minute-by-Minute*, Paul Thompson (in *The New Pearl Harbor*).

– After the events, Russian President Putin stated:

> [...] in August, "I ordered my intelligence to warn President Bush in the strongest terms that 25 terrorists were getting ready to attack the US, including important government buildings like the Pentagon." The head of Russian intelligence also said: "We had clearly warned them" on several occasions, but they "did not pay the necessary attention."[33]

– Even the Taliban, who would later be attacked in Afghanistan, warned the US:

> In late July, for example, the Taliban's Foreign Minister informed US officials that Osama bin Laden was planning a "huge attack" inside America that was imminent and would kill thousands.[34]
>
> A Moroccan agent who had penetrated al-Qaeda was evidently brought to the United States to discuss his report that bin Laden, being disappointed that the 1993 bombing had not toppled the WTC, planned "large scale operations in New York in the summer or fall of 2001."[35]

– Warnings were also reportedly given by France, Germany, Jordan, Egypt, Israel[36], who warned

---

33. MSNBC, September 15, 2001, and Agence-France-Presse, September 16, 2001, quoted in *September 11: Minute-by-Minute*, Paul Thompson (in *The New Pearl Harbor*).

34. *Independent* and Reuters, September 7, 2002, in *September 11: Minute-by-Minute*, Paul Thompson, cited in *The New Pearl Harbor*.

35. Agence-France-Presse, November 22, 2001, *International Herald Tribune*, May 21, and *London Times*, May 12, 2002, cited in *September 11: Minute-by-Minute*, Paul Thompson (in *The New Pearl Harbor*).

36. *Telegraph*, September 16, 2001, *Los Angeles Times*, September 20, 2001, Fox News, May 17, 2002, *International Herald Tribune*, May 21, 2002, and the *New York Times*, June 4, 2002, quoted in *September 11: Minute-by-Minute*, Paul Thompson (in *The New Pearl Harbor*).

a few days before 9/11 that perhaps 200 terrorists linked to Osama bin Laden were "preparing a big operation."[37]

– The United Kingdom, whose intelligence services repeatedly warned their American counterparts, sent a memo included in the President's Daily Brief (PDB) of August 6 that President Bush received while staying at his ranch in Texas. This document warned that al-Qaeda had planned attacks against the United States involving multiple airplane hijackings. Yet,

> the White House kept this warning secret, with the President repeatedly claiming after 9/11 that he had received no warning of any kind.[38]

When CBS Evening News revealed the existence of this PDB on May 15, several White House officials came forward to downplay its importance. Among them was National security adviser Condoleezza Rice, who described the August 6, 2001 Brief

> as "very vague," "very non-specific," "mostly historical," and "nothing really new here."[39]

In April 2004, President Bush stated that this

> PDB said nothing about an attack on America. It talked about intentions, about somebody who hated America—well, we

---

37. David Wastell and Philipp Jacobson, "Israeli Security Issued Warning to CIA of Large-Scale Terror Attacks," *Telegraph*, September 16, 2001, quoted in *The War on Freedom: How and Why America Was Attacked September 11, 2001*, Ahmed Nafeez Mosaddeq, Joshua Tree, Calif.: Tree of Life Publications, 2002, 114 (in *The New Pearl Harbor*).
38. *The New Pearl Harbor*, p. 71.
39. *The President's Daily Brief*, by Thomas S. Blanton, Updated April 12, 2004, The National Security Archive.

knew that. ... The question was, who was going to attack us, when and where, and with what.[40]

However, the document was titled *Bin Ladin Determined To Strike in US* and, after the White House had finally agreed to communicate it, the *New York Times* began its summary as follows—although every attempt was made to classify the document and not make it public in the name of national security:

> In a single 17-sentence document, the intelligence briefing delivered to President Bush in August 2001 spells out the who, hints at the what and points towards the where of the terrorist attacks on New York and Washington that followed 36 days later.[41]

Here is an extract from the PDB as published by the 9/11 Commission:

> The following is the text of an item from the Presidential Daily Brief received by President George W. Bush on August 6, 2001.[37] Redacted material is indicated by brackets.

> Bin Ladin Determined To Strike in US

> [...] A clandestine source said in 1998 that a Bin Ladin cell in New York was recruiting Muslim-American youth for attacks. **We have not been able to corroborate some of the more sensational threat reporting, such as that from a [−] service in 1998 saying that Bin Laden wanted to hijack a US aircraft to gain the release of "Blind Shaykh" 'Umar**

---

40. Joseph Curl, "Bush defends memo stance – 'No indication' of 9/11 attacks," The Washington Times, 12 April 2004, front page, quoted in The National Security Archive (see previous note).

41. *A Warning, but Clear? White House Tries to Make the Point That New Details Add Up to Old News*, Douglas Jehl, The New York Times, April 11, 2004.

'Abd al-Rahman and other US-held extremists.[42]
Nevertheless, FBI information since that time indicates patterns of suspicious activity in this country consistent with preparations for hijackings or other types of attacks, including recent surveillance of federal buildings in New York..[43]

Anyone can gather from what is written about these preparations that the FBI had been watching **for more than two years**, since 1998. It should also be noted that during this case, it also emerged that there had been a federal report in 1999, two years before the events,

> speculating that al-Qaida might crash a plane into either the CIA headquarters, the White House or the Pentagon. Mr. Bush's spokesman, Ari Fleischer, dismissed the report, saying it was a psychological study and not written by intelligence officers.[44]

Let us assume the improbable: the FBI had known nothing, seen nothing and heard nothing about the countless alerts from abroad. We will focus solely on the information in its possession on "preparations for hijackings or other types of attacks," such as the operation presented in the next paragraph.

The Yousef-Scarpa Story

Ramzi Yousef, considered as the architect of the attack against the WTC on February 26, 1993, was arrested in Pakistan two years later, on February 7, 1995. His extradition to the United States followed,

---

42. In bold in *The 9/11 Commission Report*.
43. *A Warning, but Clear? White House Tries to Make the Point That New Details Add Up to Old News*, Douglas Jehl, *The New York Times*, 11 April 2004.
44. *Bush insists: 'I had no warning about Sept 11'*, Matthew Engel, *The Guardian*, May 18, 2002.

where he would stand trial. Subsequently, he was incarcerated in a federal prison in Manhattan, along with his accomplices. There he met a mobster and member of a large crime family, Greg Scarpa Jr., with whom he gradually began exchanging information. Little did Yousef know, Scarpa Jr was secretly reporting this information back to the FBI, in exchange for a reduced sentence.

His interviews with FBI agents are recorded in forms FD-302[45]. Here is how Peter Lance summarizes the whole story in his book *Cover Up*[46]:

> That report was one of thirty-seven separate intelligence briefings that Greg Scarpa Jr. gave the Feds over the course of eleven months between May 5, 1996, and February 7, 1997. One of the FBI 302s, from December 30, 1996, revealed a threat by the bomb maker that if he wasn't freed, Osama bin Laden, aka "Bojinga," would order the hijacking of airliners to free Yousef's fellow al Qaeda cell members, along with blind Sheikh Omar Abdel Rahman and the other nine defendants convicted with the Sheikh in 1995 in the "Day of Terror" plot to blow up the bridges and tunnels around Manhattan.
>
> That very prediction–an airplane hijack plot to free the Sheikh–was contained in a 1998 Presidential Daily Briefing (PDB) sent to President Clinton that was one of the news-making revelations after publication of the 9/11 Commission final report. And the identical threat was included four years and eight months later in the controversial August 6, 2001 PDB* received by George W. Bush at his ranch in Crawford, Texas.

---

45. "A FD-302 form is used by FBI agents to "report or summarize the interviews that they conduct" [...]. It consists of information taken from the subject, rather than details about the subject themselves." https://en.wikipedia.org/wiki/List_of_FBI_forms.
46. *Cover Up*, Peter Lance, ReganBooks, 2004, p. 104.

This is the PDB that we briefly mentioned above. Peter Lance continues his indictment:

> The threat warnings leading up to the 9/11 attacks contained in that single PDB were considered so important by the 9/11 Commissioners that the document almost provoked a constitutional crisis when the Bush administration moved unsuccessfully to keep it classified.
>
> Now, for the first time, we have proof that the FBI was in possession of that same threat information, directly from Ramzi Yousef, in 1996—two years earlier than the earliest such intelligence cited by the 9/11 Commission.
>
> After examining them [the 302 memos], it seems clear that no one with a detailed understanding of Ramzi Yousef's bomb-making methods and post-WTC bombing terror plots could conclude that the material from Scarpa was anything but genuine.
>
> Indeed, *Daily News* reporter Greg Smith, who first broke the story of the Scarpa-Yousef relationship, reported in a September 24, 2000, story that Patrick Fitzgerald, the head of the Organized Crime and Terrorism Unit of the SDNY, submitted a sealed affidavit on June 25, 1998, in which he said that a follow up investigation "appeared to corroborate Scarpa's information."[47]
>
> But it didn't seem to matter. […] Greg Jr.'s Yousef information was called "a hoax," and he got forty years.

Even if Greg Scarpa Jr. undoubtedly deserved his heavy sentence, he was not granted leniency. This was despite the risks taken for almost a year, as well as the valuable information he collected and transmitted to the FBI, which could (should) have made it possible

47. *Terrorist Called Pals on Feds Line*, Greg B. Smith, *New York Daily News*, September 24, 2000, quoted in *Cover Up*, p. 105.

to prevent September 11. He was then confined to the ADX High Security Penitentiary in Florence, Colorado, where Ramzi Yousef and his accomplices were also incarcerated. Here is how Peter Lance summarizes the situation:

> The government faced a critical choice: to embrace Greg Scarpa Jr., or to cut him loose; to reveal the extraordinary leads he had received in his contact with Yousef, or to bury them in order to keep a string of mob cases from falling apart. The choice would be made at the highest levels of the Justice Department.
> And in the end—as happened at so many other points along the road to 9/11—America's national security would be sacrificed in favor of political convenience.
> Faced with choosing the war on terror over organized crime, the FBI and the Justice Department decided to go with the mob.[48]

When *Cover Up* was published, on the third anniversary of 9/11, Peter Lance wrote an article with a meaningful conclusion:

> As I looked back on the Justice Department's counter-terrorism track record, I concluded that many of the dots left unconnected by the FBI and DOJ on the road to 9/11 appeared to have been the result of an intentional obscuring of the evidence. Continuing to work sources and examine the reams of documentary evidence generated in the SDNY [Southern District of New York] al Qaeda cases, I came to the conclusion that the FBI's failure to prevent the African embassy bombings in 1998, the deadly assault on U.S.S. *Cole* in 2000, and the 9/11 attacks themselves, went beyond gross negligence.[49]

---

48. Cover *Up*, p. 95.
49. *Greg Scarpa Jr. A Mafia wiseguy uncovers a treasure trove of al Qaeda intel*, Peter Lance, http://peterlance.com/wordpress/?p=682.

He adds:

> But many unanswered questions remained. I wanted to know the names of the men and women in the shadows at Justice who had suppressed the evidence and hidden the truth behind al Qaeda all those years. I also wanted to learn why the Bush 43 Administration would act to obstruct an investigation into the destruction of the Able Danger intel, a scandal that took place during the Clinton years?
> It took me months of further digging before the depth of the government's deception started to become clear.

Able Danger, another example?

According to Wikipedia[50],

> Able Danger was a classified military planning effort led by the U.S. Special Operations Command (SOCOM) and the Defense Intelligence Agency (DIA). It was created as a result of a directive from the Joint Chiefs of Staff in early October 1999 by Chairman of the Joint Chiefs of Staff Hugh Shelton, to develop an information operations campaign plan against transnational terrorism.
> According to statements by Lt. Col.Anthony Shaffer and those of four others, Able Danger had identified 2 of 3 Al Qaeda cells active in the 9/11 attacks; the "Brooklyn cell" linked to "Blind Sheik" Omar Abdel-Rahman, including September 11 attacks leader Mohamed Atta, and three of the 9/11 plot's other 19 hijackers.

The revelation of this information was so crucial that it triggered a formal investigation. Appropriately, the US Senate Intelligence

---

50. https://en.wikipedia.org/wiki/Able_Danger

Committee was created, which conducted a sixteen-month investigation before stating in December 2006:

> Able Danger did not identify Mohamed Atta or any other 9/11 hijacker at any time prior to September 11, 2001.

And Wikipedia adds:

> [...] and dismissed other assertions that have fueled 9/11 conspiracy theories.

Another investigation was initiated by the Department of Defense and to the Inspector General's (IG) Office. In September 2006, three months before the US Senate Intelligence Committee, this report came to the same conclusions that:

> A. The anti-terrorist program, Able Danger, did not identify Mohamed Atta or any of the other 9/11 terrorists before the 9/11 attack.
> B. Able Danger members were not prohibited from sharing intelligence information with law enforcement authorities or other agencies that could have acted on that information. In fact, Able Danger produced no actionable intelligence information.[51]

Nevertheless, Wikipedia's article reads:

> However, some of the people questioned by the IG claimed their statements to the IG were distorted by investigators in the final IG's report, and the report omitted essential information that they had provided. Lt. Col. Tony Shaffer has claimed that

---

51. Report of Investigation, Office of the Inspector General, Department of Defense, September 18, 2006, p. 89.

the DOD retaliated against him for speaking out publicly about the IG report's distortions.

It is difficult to know where the truth lies since the military decided to destroy all data of the program. Nevertheless, Lt. Col. Anthony Shaffer confirmed his statements to French journalist François Bringer, who interviewed him for his book[52]:

The ten people making up this "cell" to whom Shaffer refers are of course not the same as that of the Blind Sheikh's cell, which had been dismantled after the 1993 attack. The cell Shaffer brought up today is another, which also operated in Brooklyn, long after the '93 attack. It is the one of the 9/11 hijackers. That of Mohammed Atta and his eighteen accomplices whom Able Danger had spotted as early as 1999, two years before the attacks! An incredible discovery...

Later, Lt. Col. Shaffer reveals that

Atta was discovered through information collected by what we call our "mosque effort."

This covers all the intelligence collected in the field, because

we took information from the Internet, everything found on social networks, but we also had information about those who frequented certain mosques. We had "researchers" who would go to the mosques to find out who came and when they came. Often, we were able to get the welcome books from these mosques, which are easily available, we also bought commercial databases. Airline and credit card databases.

---

52. François Bringer, *Ils avaient donné l'alerte – Whistle-blowers, ces agents qu'on a fait taire*, éditions du Toucan, 2011, p. 25 et seq.

Everything we could buy, we bought. We were trying to spot new affiliations, travel habits. The best thing is when it could be confirmed that an individual from one of the groups was meeting a "known" terrorist. This allowed us to confirm a link between the known terrorist and the one we suspected, helping us confirm the identities of the "bad guys."[53]

He continues:

...we knew that there were active al-Qaeda cells in the United States. We knew it as early as 1999. Individuals operated according to a pattern of typical terrorist cells and these cells were linked to al-Qaeda.

This information was a bomb for the government, and I know it landed on President Clinton's desk, inserted in the Millennium Report. The United States was on red alert in 1999, fearing an attack on the Year 2000 celebrations. But there, no one saw fit to do anything with it; so that is the first thing: there are terrorist cells here and now, and we do nothing...

... and that, in my opinion, is the biggest wrench that has been put in the works of Able Danger. We had a relatively clear indication that a plot was being prepared, that something was developing.

That is why we tried to bypass the Pentagon and give this information directly to the Department of Justice, because, at the time, in the United States, only Justice was authorized to deal with criminals within our borders. The Pentagon, on the other hand, had no legal weapons or legal authority. And so, this was the biggest obstacle we faced: we were NEVER allowed to pass on this information to anyone who could have used it.[54]

---

53. *Ils avaient donné l'alerte – Whistle-blowers, ces agents qu'on a fait taire*, p. 38.
54. *Ils avaient donné l'alerte – Whistle-blowers, ces agents qu'on a fait taire*, p. 42.

François Bringer then asked him if it would have been possible to circumvent the law and break this famous "wall" between intelligence agencies. Here is the answer:

> I tried three times with my WFO contact, the Washington Field Office, the FBI's operational branch in the capital, to arrange meetings between the special forces, the members of Able Danger and the WFO unit in charge of collecting information on al-Qaeda cells. The problem is that the Pentagon lawyers were totally against these appointments and cancelled them as I set them up. In fact, none of them ever took place.[55]

Therefore, it is not the FBI's fault that these meetings did not happen. Was there no other solution?

> I had contacts within the FBI because I worked for them from time to time as an undercover agent. So, I went to my colleagues and tried to tell them that they really had to see our data. But the FBI wasn't interested either.[56]

It is unbelievable that none of these FBI agents even considered that it could be useful to look at the data. They were familiar with Lt. Col. Shaffer and he had obviously insisted. Moreover, he adds in the interview:

> Even Louis Freeh, the former director of the FBI, said, "If I had received, while I was still in office, the information from Able Danger, I could have prevented 9/11." These are his own words, he even wrote an editorial in the *Wall Street Journal*. "And I," said Shaffer, "feel the same."[57]

---

55. *Ils avaient donné l'alerte – Whistle-blowers, ces agents qu'on a fait taire*, p. 46.
56. *Ils avaient donné l'alerte – Whistle-blowers, ces agents qu'on a fait taire*, p. 46.
57. *Ils avaient donné l'alerte – Whistle-blowers, ces agents qu'on a fait taire*, p. 45.

We are not convinced that Louis Freeh, the director of the FBI from September 1993 to June 2001, was in the best position to make such statements. This book shows that he and his services had several opportunities to prevent 9/11 and yet the terrorists still achieved their goal. However, his editorial is interesting, especially for his opinion regarding the 9/11 Commission:

> The Able Danger intelligence, if confirmed, is undoubtedly the most relevant fact of the entire post-9/11 inquiry. Even the most junior investigator would immediately know that the name and photo ID of Atta in 2000 is precisely the kind of tactical intelligence the FBI has many times employed to prevent attacks and arrest terrorists. Yet the 9/11 Commission inexplicably concluded that it "was not historically significant." This astounding conclusion—in combination with the failure to investigate Able Danger and incorporate it into its findings—raises serious challenges to the commission's credibility and, if the facts prove out, might just render the commission historically insignificant itself.[58]

If a former FBI director says so...

François Bringer subsequently asked Lt. Col. Shaffer about the 9/11 Commission. He had personally met Philip Zelikow, the Executive Director, who had asked him for a meeting as soon as he was in Washington because his testimony was "crucial." But he would not receive him, or even answer his calls. François Bringer then reported that Anthony Shaffer

> would later learn from a Congressional representative, who had demanded to know why Able Danger had not been "retained"

---

58. *An Incomplete Investigation, Why did the 9/11 Commission Ignore "Able Danger"?*, Louis Freeh, *Wall Street Journal*, November, 17, 2005.

in the Commission, that a member of the Commission had this Orwellian answer: "The facts about Able Danger did not meet the criteria of the story we wanted to tell..."[59]

It is a strange answer.
Of course, the fact that Lt Col Anthony Shaffer dared speak out against the government version shattered his career.
François Bringer recounts the end of their interview:

> What have you learned from all these years of hardship? He is sitting in his leather armchair, his hands behind his head. A time of pause, then comes a serene glow in his grey eyes. "In Washington, the truth is negotiable!"[60]

---

59. *Ils avaient donné l'alerte – Whistle-blowers, ces agents qu'on a fait taire*, p. 67.
60. *Ils avaient donné l'alerte – Whistle-blowers, ces agents qu'on a fait taire*, p. 75.

Chapter 9/3

The FBI Knew, Part 2
Kamikazes and Trainee Pilots

Statements from the Top

Moments after the attacks, President George W. Bush stated that:

> Nobody in our government at least, and I don't think the prior government, could have foreseen flying air planes into buildings.

Condoleezza Rice claimed something similar:

> No-one could have predicted that they would try to use an airplane as a missile.

The Washington Post was interested in the question and interviewed U.S. Air Force generals:

> As new details emerged yesterday about the military's initial reactions to Tuesday's terrorist attacks, they revealed just how ill-prepared the Pentagon was—not only to protect itself but also to guard U.S. skies and American lives against commercial airliners turned into deadly weapons.
> Three Air Force generals, all sharing some responsibility for America's air defense, described in interviews how inadequate the procedures were for dealing with what was occurring. "This was something we had never seen before, something we had never even thought of," one said.[61]

---

61. *Pentagon was unprepared for attack*, Bradley Graham, *The Washington Post*, September 16, 2001.

"Never even thought of?" Maybe this should be put into perspective: Japanese suicide bombers threw their planes at the Navy during the Second World War. As we also pointed out in the previous chapter, a group linked to Al-Qaida attempted to crash an aircraft into the Eiffel Tower in 1994 and made the cover of *Time* in January 1995, not to mention other similar attempts elsewhere. So, was it really something they had "never seen before"?

These statements by the highest political and military authorities therefore appear to have little credibility. So, let us turn to the FBI and see if, despite the statements by its director Robert S. Mueller that there were no warning signs, this threat also remained unknown to one of the world's best anti-terrorism agencies during the years leading up to September 11.

Repeated Warnings

We will rely mainly on Chapter 1—*Warning Signs* of *The Terror Timeline* and its more than sixty pages. Only titles on the subject of aircraft used as weapons will be included, sometimes with clarifications provided by Paul Thompson and his team and/or with our comments.

1993 (B): Early Evidence of Osama's Interest
in Airplanes and Training Pilots (p. 10).
Bin Laden buys a jet from the U.S. military in Arizona. It will be used to transport missiles from Pakistan that kill American Special Forces in Somalia. Some of his followers begin training in U.S. flight schools.

1993 (C): Expert Panel Predicts Terrorists Will Use Planes
as Weapons on Symbolic U.S. Targets (p. 10).
The information is not published in their report *Terror 2000*, but later, in 1994, by one of them in *Futurist Magazine*. The World Trade Center is mentioned as an example of target.

This means that there were seven (long) years before September 11 to anticipate. It is noteworthy that this panel was convened at the request of the Pentagon, so there must be someone in the army who was aware of the information.

February 1995: Bojinka "Second Wave" Fully Revealed to Philippines Investigators; Information Given to U.S. (p. 13).

As a reminder, this phase consisted of hijacking commercial aircraft and crashing them into American buildings. The terrorist turned informant Abdul Hakim Murad revealed the targets: the headquarters of the CIA, the Pentagon, an unidentified nuclear plant, the World Trade Center, the Transamerica Tower in San Francisco, and the former Sears Tower in Chicago ("Willis Tower" since 2009). This revelation was made six years before 9/11, and it is the exact description of the attacks.

1996: FBI Fumbles Flight School Investigations (p. 16).
[…] Apparently, the FBI closes the investigation when they fail to find any other potential suspects. (*Insight*, 5/27/02).

January 1996: Muslim Extremists Plan Suicide Attack on White House (p. 16).
U.S. intelligence obtains information concerning a suicide attack on the White House planned by individuals connected with Sheikh Omar Abdul-Rahman and a key al-Qaeda operative. The plan is to fly from Afghanistan to the U.S. and crash into the White House. (9/11 Congressional Inquiry, 9/18/02).

July 6-August 11, 1996: "Atlanta Rules" Established
to Protect Against Terrorists Using Planes
as Flying Weapons (p. 17)

U.S. officials identify crop dusters and suicide flights as potential terrorist weapons that could threaten the Olympic Games in Atlanta, Georgia. They take steps to prevent any air attacks. [...] Law enforcement agents also fan out to regional airports throughout northern Georgia "to make sure nobody hijacked a small aircraft and tried to attack one of the venues," says Woody Johnson, the FBI agent in charge. Counterterrorism "tsar" Richard Clarke uses this same security blanket approach to other major events, referring to the approach as "Atlanta Rules." (*Chicago Tribune*, 11/18/01; *Wall Street Journal*, 4/1/04; *Against All Enemies*, by Richard Clarke, 3/04, pp. 108-09).

With all the above information available, is it still possible to claim that "no-one could have predicted that they would try to use an airplane as a missile" as was declared by Condoleezza Rice, despite her role as National Security Advisor, and so many other influential figures? Did nobody in the Bush Administration, or at least those in charge of national security, know the Atlanta Rules? The American people trusted these "professionals" with their lives. Unfortunately, the list of warnings will go on much further, and it is not even exhaustive:

May 15, 1998: Oklahoma FBI Memo Warns
of Potential Terrorist-Related Flight Training;
No Investigation Ensues (p. 20).

This was one of the documents sent by field offices concerned about the high number of trainee pilots coming from the Middle-East. At least three 9/11 terrorists trained there: Mohamed Atta, Marwan Alshehhi and Zacarias Moussaoui.

After May 15, 1998: FBI Again Ignores Warnings About
Terrorists Planning to Obtain U.S. Pilot Training (p. 20).
The FBI receives reports that a terrorist organization might
be planning to bring students to the U.S. for flight training,
at some point in 1998 after the May 15 memo warns about
possible terrorists training at U.S. flight schools. (*New York
Daily News*, 9/25/02). The FBI is aware that people connected
to this unnamed organization have performed surveillance
and security tests at airports in the U.S. and made comments
suggesting an intention to target civil aviation. Apparently, this
warning is not shared with other FBI offices or the FAA, and a
connection with the Oklahoma warning is not made; a similar
warning will follow in 1999. (9/11 Congressional Inquiry,
7/24/03).

August 1998: CIA Warns That Terrorists Plan to Fly
Bomb-Laden Plane into WTC (p. 21).

Late August 1998: Al-Qaeda Planning U.S. Attack,
but Not Yet Ready (p. 21).
The FBI learns that al-Qaeda is planning an attack on the
U.S., but "things are not ready yet. We don't have everything
prepared," according to a captured member of the al-Qaeda
cell that bombed the U.S. embassy in Kenya. (*USA Today*,
8/29/02).

September 1998: Bin Laden's Next Operations May
Involve Crashing Airplane into U.S. Airport (p. 22).
U.S. intelligence uncovers information that bin Laden's next
operation could possibly involve crashing with explosives
into a U.S. airport. This information is provided to senior U.S.
officials. (9/11 Congressional Inquiry, 9/18/02; *Washington
Post*, 9/19/02).

October 8, 1998: FAA Warns of al-Qaeda Threat
to U.S. Civil Aviation (p. 22).
[...] It specifically warns against a possible terrorist hijacking
"at a metropolitan airport in the Eastern United States." [...].
(*Boston Globe*, 5/26/02).

Autumn 1998: Rumors of bin Laden Plot Involving Aircraft
in New York and Washington Surface Again (p. 22).

1999: British Intelligence Warns al-Qaeda Plans
to Use Aircraft, Possibly as Flying Bombs (p. 23).

1999: FBI Learns of Terrorists' Plans to Send Students
to U.S. for Aviation Training; Investigation
Opportunity Bungled (p. 23).

This last warning was similar to the previous year's. In September 1999,

> "Suicide bomber belonging to Al Qaeda's Martyrdom Battalion," went the report to the National Intelligence Council, "could crash-land an aircraft packed with high explosives into the Pentagon, the headquarters of the C.I.A. or the White House." [...].
> However, that report was from the Library of Congress, dated September 1999. Bill Clinton was the president who sat on it for 16 months and did nothing, ostensibly because it was not deemed "actionable."[62]

February-July 2001: Trial Presents FBI with Information
About Pilot Training Scheme (p. 30).
[...] Testimony reveals that two bin Laden operatives had

62. *The Williams Memo*, William Safire, *The New York Times*, May 20, 2002.

received pilot training in Texas and Oklahoma and another had been asked to take lessons. One bin Laden aide becomes a government witness and gives the FBI detailed information about a pilot training scheme. This new information does not lead to any new FBI investigations into the matter. (*Washington Post*, 9/23/01).

March 4, 2001: Television Show Eerily
Envisions 9/11 Attacks (p. 30).
Contradicting the later claim that no one could have envisioned the 9/11 attacks, a short-lived Fox television program called *The Lone Gunmen* airs a pilot episode in which terrorists try to fly an airplane into the WTC. The heroes save the day and the airplane narrowly misses the building.

June 2001: Germans Warn of Plan to Use Aircraft
as Missiles on U.S, and Israeli Symbols (p. 35).

June 20, 2001: *Time Magazine* Mentions al-Qaeda
Using Planes as Weapons (p. 37).

This operation would take place during the G8 Summit in Genoa, Italy, and aimed to assassinate President Bush, among other leaders of the "free world."

July 10, 2001: FBI Agent Sends Memo Warning
That "Inordinate Number" of Muslim Extremists
Are Learning to Fly in Arizona (pp. 39-41).

This is the widely known "Phoenix Memo" to which we will come back later.

July 31, 2001: FAA Issues General Hijacking Warning (p. 42).

After but a few examples, does the U.S. Air Force general's claim that "This was something we had never seen before, something we had never even thought of" hold the slightest bit of credibility? In any case, the FBI cannot claim that it was impossible to imagine since they regularly received alerts about exactly this type of operation in the years preceding 9/11.

Keep in mind that we have only presented titles involving terrorists and aircraft. There were many other alerts—not explicitly referring to air attacks—issued by American intelligence about bin Laden and al-Qaeda.

The "Phoenix Memo"

This document has caused a lot of ink to flow in the United States, showing almost by itself that intelligence agencies failed in preventing September 11. One could suggest that it was rather used as a smokescreen, an excuse saying, "but if we had received this document, we could have prevented September 11!" It may also have been an attempt to mask the responsibility, guilt and complicity which we have yet to address. It has also served to strengthen the American security apparatus, an objective achieved to an almost oversized extent.

Briefly put, Agent Kenneth Williams from the FBI office in Phoenix, Arizona, sent a five-page memorandum by email to six recipients at headquarters (at the unit investigating bin Laden and radical fundamentalism) and two at the New York office on July 10, 2001. The document concerned Middle Eastern men suspiciously taking piloting lessons in the region. They were connected to a Chechen al-Qaeda-affiliated terrorist group. He thought this could be part of bin Laden's plan to train pilots to hijack planes and made several recommendations, including sharing information with the intelligence community.

No reaction came from the recipients. *The New York Times* provided an explanation:

> Usually, internal investigative proposals that involve agency-wide resources are reviewed by high F.B.I. officials. But in this case F.B.I. officials have said that officials who read the memorandum were distracted by other cases, a plot against American interests in France and the investigation of the attack in October 2000 on the destroyer *Cole*.[63]

While the threat from al-Qaeda was becoming increasingly specific and imminent, FBI officials were otherwise occupied, notably with the attack on the USS *Cole* which had been committed by none other than al-Qaeda. Therefore, the explanation above seems paradoxical.

Agent Williams was not aware of the warnings about bin Laden, including hijackings targeting mainly New York and Washington. However, here is what he testified a year later at the Senate Judiciary Committee:

> [...] he believed that if the bureau had implemented his recommendation to interview hundreds, if not thousands, of Middle Eastern students at American flight schools, the effort would not have thwarted the Sept. 11 attacks on the World Trade Center and the Pentagon, said lawmakers who attended the session.[64]

That is exactly what we think: The Phoenix Memo could not have prevented 9/11 if the will to act upon it was lacking. As will be proven, however, the FBI had more information that could have

---

63. *Ashcroft Learned of Agent's Alert Just After 9/11*, by David Johnston and Don Van Natta Jr., *The New York Times*, May 21, 2002.
64. *Anti-U.S. Views at Pilot Schools Prompted Agent's Alert*, by Don Van Natta Jr. and David Johnston, *The New York Times*, May 22, 2002.

prevented the tragedy. Let us start with Niaz Khan, whose story is far less common knowledge than Agent Williams's memo.

"Return Him to London and Forget About It."

Niaz Khan was a thirty-year-old British citizen originally from Pakistan. Overwhelmed by gambling debts, he was offered help by two mysterious men at the exit of a casino in Manchester. In exchange, he should provide services to al-Qaeda. He accepted, received several thousand dollars and was flown to Lahore, Pakistan, where he waited in a hotel for further instructions. From there he was blindfolded and taken to a house. Here is how NBC News reports his testimony about what happened later:

> [...] at the Lahore training compound, he and up to 30 other men were taught hijacking basics, including how to smuggle guns and other weapons through airport security, techniques to overpower passengers and crew and how to get into a cockpit.
>
> [...] After about a week of training, Khan said he was given money to fly a circuitous route from Pakistan to Doha, Qatar, to London, to Zurich, Switzerland, back to London, and then off to New York. The purpose, he said, was to allow him to observe flight operations and on-board security measures.
>
> Upon landing at JFK airport, Khan says he was supposed to go to a taxi stand, find a man in a white prayer cap and use a code.[65]
>
> "They said I would live there for a while and meet some other people and we would hijack a plane from JFK and fly it into a building." (*London Times*, 5/9/04).[66]

---

65. *Did al-Qaida Trainee Warn FBI Before 9/11?*, by Lisa Myers and the NBC Investigative Unit, NBC News, updated 7/26/2004.
66. *The Terror Timeline*, p. 27.

Niaz Khan had other ideas: he took a bus to Atlantic City where he gambled away the money given to him by al-Qaeda. Afraid he would be killed for betrayal, he turned himself in to the FBI where he explained the whole story.

> For three weeks, FBI counterterrorism agents in Newark, New Jersey interview him. (MSNBC, 6/3/04; *Observer*, 6/6/04). One FBI agent recalls, "We were incredulous. Flying a plane into a building sounded crazy but we polygraphed him, and he passed." (*London Times*, 5/9/04). A former FBI official says the FBI agents believed Khan, and pursued every lead in the case, but word came from FBI headquarters saying, "Return him to London and forget about it."[67]

He was returned to Britain and handed over to British authorities. However, the British interviewed him only for about two hours, and then released him. The FBI agent in charge of Niaz Khan will later say:

> I just assumed that when Niaz was turned over, the British authorities would have conducted a full investigation. What I would have done is re-inserted him into the community and worked him.... We know that didn't happen. It's a real shame. [Vanity Fair, 11/2004].[68]

Here is how it ended:

> Khan remains surprised that, to this day, the FBI, CIA and Scotland Yard have never asked for his help in identifying the street address of the Lahore safe house where he and dozens of other men were trained. He says he saw some identifying

---

67. *The Terror Timeline*, p. 27.
68. http://www.historycommons.org/entity.jsp?entity=niaz_khan

signs and might be able to locate it today. "I am just surprised because [they] never came back to ask some more things," he said. "[The FBI] believed me, but maybe not seriously."[69]

The FBI has more surprises in store.

FBI vs. FBI—Minneapolis

This is definitely one of the more famous stories about the FBI and September 11, so we will be brief.

On August 16, 2001, the Minneapolis office, where Colleen Rowley worked as Special Agent and Chief Division Counsel, received a phone call from Pan Am Flight School. One of their students, Zacarias Moussaoui, had raised their suspicions and they were suspecting that he was a terrorist preparing to crash a plane into a city.

The Bureau decided to send a team while Colleen notified the Radical Fundamentalism Unit (RFU), a division within the FBI that deals with radical Islamism. While it may seem strange, the RFU advised not to make the arrest. In the meantime, Minneapolis discovered that the suspect's visa had expired.

After a final telephone conversation with the RFU which confirmed its previous order, Agent Harry Samit disregarded it and arrested Zacarias Moussaoui in his motel room. Hussein Al Attash, also present, was scooped up in the process. Computers were seized, but Moussaoui refused to let his be opened.

It was therefore necessary to obtain a warrant from a judge through the FBI's hierarchical channel. Colleen sent a long report to headquarters for exactly this purpose. Here is how François Bringer tells the story after interviewing her:

---

69. *Did al-Qaida Trainee Warn FBI Before 9/11?*, by Lisa Myers and the NBC Investigative Unit, NBC News, updated 7/26/2004.

Three days pass by, her supervisor contacts her to tell her that she doesn't have enough evidence for her warrant. He advised her not to "be stubborn" about it.

It is mystifying: why did he ask her not to "be stubborn"? Did he want to protect Moussaoui? For what reason?
Colleen decided not to give up on the case:

She was amazed by the obstacles suddenly put in her way and felt like time was of the essence in the Moussaoui case. While preparing another report, she contacted her former "correspondents" in French intelligence, an action at the very limit of her power.[70]

Indeed, she had been stationed in Paris and spoke French. The allied service responded and informed her that they had been monitoring Moussaoui for several years. He was in contact with terrorists and had fought in Chechnya under the orders of an Osama bin Laden companion. He even allegedly participated in organizing the hijacking of the Air France Algiers-Paris flight in 1994, the objective of which had been to crash the plane into the Eiffel Tower.

With this, what would usually be considered crucial information, she sent a new report, but the warrant still did not come. She would later discover that critical data she submitted had been deleted by her hierarchy before relaying the request. Otherwise, based on the information provided, she would very likely have received a positive response from the judge. Why delete this information from her report, except to prevent her from obtaining the requested warrant to search the computer? The *New York Times* offered a different explanation:

---

70. *Ils avaient donné l'alerte*, François Bringer, p. 132.

> Intimidated by the brouhaha about supposed ethnic profiling of Wen Ho Lee, lawyers at John Ashcroft's Justice Department wanted no part of going after this Arab.[71]

This is difficult to believe for the sole reason that

> F.B.I. Washington bureaucrats were, in agent Rowley's words, "consistently, almost deliberately thwarting the Minneapolis F.B.I. agents' efforts."[72]

Admittedly, the Wen Ho Lee case had major repercussions in the United States, but the explanation given later comes off as weak in the Moussaoui affair due to the following facts: there was information from French intelligence confirming his links to members of al-Qaeda, his participation in Chechnya and even possible collusion in the hijacking of the Air France flight.

Once more: why delete this information from Colleen Rowley's report? The Phoenix Memo had been received some weeks earlier at headquarters. These two reports combined provided sufficient material for a high alert. Adding to this was all the intelligence sent to Washington on the increasing likelihood of an al-Qaeda attack on American territory, almost certainly by hijacking planes and crashing them in Washington and New York.

If Moussaoui's computer had been analyzed—it would be done after 9/11—perhaps the attacks could have been prevented, as its data confirmed his presence in Chechnya, his links to eleven of the future hijackers, money transfer receipts from the al-Qaeda cell in Hamburg, etc.

While waiting for the much-needed warrant, the Minneapolis team continued the investigation. It discovered that its detainee had also filed a flight plan to New York's Kennedy Airport during his training.

---

71. *The Rowley Memo*, William Safire, *The New York Times*, May 27, 2002.
72. *The Rowley Memo*, William Safire, *The New York Times*, May 27, 2002.

For what purpose?

> One of the agents assumes that he will try to hijack or crash a plane onto this airport. In the notes he took during this meeting, another wrote in the margin of his notebook: "Maybe he wants to fly a plane into the World Trade Center?" These notes were recorded in a report now in the hands of the 9/11 Commission.[73]

What then pushed Colleen Rowley into the uncomfortable world of whistleblowers were the repeated statements by the new FBI Director, Robert S. Mueller, who claimed as soon as he could that the Bureau knew nothing that could have prevented the events. On May 21, 2002, she sent him a letter and addressed a copy to the Congressional Oversight Committee to protect herself. This was probably how the letter reached the media, which triggered a storm. In it she basically accused him of misstating the facts as he repeatedly declared after September 11 that the FBI had known nothing that could have prevented the hijackings.
Here is how she began her 13-page letter[74]:

> Dear Director Mueller:
>
> I feel at this point that I have to put my concerns in writing concerning the important topic of the FBI's response to evidence of terrorist activity in the United States prior to September 11th. The issues are fundamentally ones of INTEGRITY and go to the heart of the FBI's law enforcement mission and mandate. Moreover, at this critical juncture in fashioning future policy to promote the most effective handling

---

73. *Ils avaient donné l'alerte*, François Bringer, p. 136.
74. Coleen Rowley's Memo to FBI Director Robert Mueller, May 21, 2002, http://www.apfn.org/apfn/WTC_whistleblower1.htm.

of ongoing and future threats to United States citizens' security, it is of absolute importance that an unbiased, completely accurate picture emerge of the FBI's current investigative and management strengths and failures.

To get to the point, I have deep concerns that a delicate and subtle shading/skewing of facts by you and others at the highest levels of FBI management has occurred and is occurring. The term "cover up" would be too strong a characterization which is why I am attempting to carefully (and perhaps over laboriously) choose my words here. I base my concerns on my relatively small, peripheral but unique role in the Moussaoui investigation in the Minneapolis Division prior to, during and after September 11th and my analysis of the comments I have heard both inside the FBI (originating, I believe, from you and other high levels of management) as well as your Congressional testimony and public comments.

I feel that certain facts, including the following, have, up to now, been omitted, downplayed, glossed over and/or mis-characterized in an effort to avoid or minimize personal and/or institutional embarrassment on the part of the FBI and/or perhaps even for improper political reasons.

She continued her indictment with various points concerning the Moussaoui investigation. Eventually in point number 5 she says:

5) The fact is that key FBIHQ personnel whose job it was to assist and coordinate with field division agents on terrorism investigations and the obtaining and use of FISA searches (and who theoretically were privy to many more sources of intelligence information than field division agents), continued to, almost inexplicably[5], throw up roadblocks and undermine Minneapolis's by-now desperate efforts to obtain a FISA search warrant, long after the French intelligence service

provided its information and probable cause became clear. HQ personnel brought up almost ridiculous questions in their apparent efforts to undermine the probable cause[6]. In all of their conversations and correspondence, HQ personnel never disclosed to the Minneapolis agents that the Phoenix Division had, only approximately three weeks earlier, warned of Al Qaeda operatives in flight schools seeking flight training for terrorist purposes!

These are serious accusations against Headquarters, but it did not end there:

Nor did FBIHQ personnel do much to disseminate the information about Moussaoui to other appropriate intelligence/ law enforcement authorities. When, in a desperate 11th hour measure to bypass the FBIHQ roadblock, the Minneapolis Division undertook to directly notify the CIA's Counter Terrorist Center (CTC), FBIHQ personnel actually chastised the Minneapolis agents for making the direct notification without their approval!

Despite this, the 9/11 Commission's Report still dared to claim, as we pointed out in Chapter 1:

Most agents who reached management ranks had little counterterrorism experience. Second, priorities were driven at the local level by the field offices, whose concerns centered on traditional crimes such as white-collar offenses and those pertaining to drugs and gangs. Individual field offices made choices to serve local priorities, not national priorities.

In Minneapolis, to avoid a national terrorism disaster, agents stood up against their hierarchy and took career-threatening risks by contacting agencies outside the chain of command, such as the CIA (CTC) but also the FAA and the Secret Service (that did not answer). We even learn that

> An agent at the FBI headquarters' Radical Fundamentalist Unit (RFU) tells the FBI Minnesota office supervisor that the supervisor is getting people "spun up" over Zacarias Moussaoui. The supervisor replies that he is trying to get people at FBI headquarters "spun up" because he is trying to make sure that Moussaoui does "not take control of a plane and fly it into the World Trade Center." He later alleges the headquarters agent replies, "[T]hat's not going to happen. We don't know he's a terrorist. You don't have enough to show he is a terrorist. You have a guy interested in this type of aircraft– that is it." (9/11 Congressional Inquiry, 10/17/02).[75]

Incidentally, he fought in Chechnya under an al-Qaeda commander close to bin Laden and was later referred to as the "20th September 11 hijacker." Indeed, "that is it."

Colleen Rowley's letter ends with several notes, including N° 5 (from point 5 above):

> 5) During the early aftermath of September 11th, when I happened to be recounting the pre-September 11th events concerning the Moussaoui investigation to other FBI personnel in other divisions or in FBIHQ, almost everyone's first question was "Why? Why would an FBI agent(s) deliberately sabotage a case?"

It is, indeed, unbelievable. Even more so as it was not their only "investigative success," as will later be demonstrated. Colleen added:

---

75. *The Terror Timeline*, p. 220.

(I know I shouldn't be flippant about this, but jokes were actually made that the key FBIHQ personnel had to be spies or moles [...] who were actually working for Osama Bin Laden to have so undercut Minneapolis' effort.)

Not to mention other FBI field offices…
Here is the footnote N° 6, also from point 5 above:

6) For example, at one point, the Supervisory Special Agent at FBIHQ posited that the French information could be worthless because it only identified Zacarias Moussaoui by name and he, the SSA, didn't know how many people by that name existed in France. A Minneapolis agent attempted to surmount that problem by quickly phoning the FBI's legal Attache (Legat) in Paris, France, so that a check could be made of the French telephone directories. Although the Legat in France did not have access to all of the French telephone directories, he was able to quickly ascertain that there was only one listed in the Paris directory. It is not known if this sufficiently answered the question, for the SSA continued to find new reasons to stall.

How is it possible that Director Mueller, upon reading this letter, did not initiate an investigation to discover the culprits—the criminals?—guilty of blocking the Minneapolis office?

Colleen Rowley would receive *Time Magazine*'s prestigious award, shared with two other whistleblowers—Cynthia Cooper (WorldCom) and Sherron Watkins (Enron)—for "Person of the Year" of 2002.

Here is an excerpt from Wikipedia's additional information on this case:

At Moussaoui's sentencing trial, FBI agent Greg Jones testified that prior to the attacks, he urged his supervisor, Michael

Maltbie, "to prevent Zacarias Moussaoui from flying a plane into the World Trade Center". Maltbie had refused to act on 70 requests from another agent, Harry Samit, to obtain a warrant to search Moussaoui's computer.[22][76]

Let us conclude the section with the Minneapolis Division's own Harry Samit, the FBI agent who arrested Zacarias Moussaoui weeks before Sept. 11, who

told a federal jury Monday that his own superiors were guilty of "criminal negligence and obstruction" for blocking his attempts to learn whether the terrorist was part of a larger cell about to hijack planes in the United States.[77]

And he continues:

[...] as Washington kept telling him there was "no urgency and no threat," his FBI superiors sent him on "wild goose chases." For a while, Samit said, they did not even believe Moussaoui was the same person whom French intelligence sources had identified as a Muslim extremist. Samit said that FBI headquarters wanted him and his fellow agents to spend days poring through Paris phone books to make sure they had the right Moussaoui.

[...] when he asked permission to place an Arabic-speaking federal officer as a plant inside Moussaoui's cell to find out what Moussaoui was up to, Washington said no.

[...] when he prepared a lengthy memo about Moussaoui for Federal Aviation Administration officials, Washington deleted

76. [22] Markon, Jerry and Timothy Dwyer. *Damning evidence highlights FBI bungles*. Archived March 9, 2016, at the Wayback Machine. *The Sydney Morning Herald* (March 22, 2006), https://en.wikipedia.org/wiki/Zacarias_Moussaoui
77. *Special Agent Harry Samit: This American Hero is the Real Jack Bauer*, Debbie Schlussel, www.debbieschlussel.com, March 21, 2006.

key sections, including a part connecting Moussaoui with Al Qaeda leader Osama bin Laden.

Unsurprisingly, here is how the Office of the Inspector General of the Department of Justice concluded its 2004 report about the FBI handling of the Moussaoui case:

> In sum, we did not find that any employees committed intentional misconduct, or violated established FBI policies or practices, or attempted to deliberately sabotage the Moussaoui case.[78]

The systematic erasing of data linking Moussaoui to bin Laden, since this is also what the FBI hierarchy did when requesting the initial warrant, therefore did not violate "established FBI policies or practices." Interesting, especially from the top investigative agency in the United States.

Furthermore, to our knowledge this fundamental question has never been answered: why did the FBI hierarchy delete the crucial information about the link between Moussaoui and bin Laden? It is reasonable to suggest that 9/11 may have been avoided without these deletions, even if most authorities claim otherwise. To the latter must be added other information that points in the same direction, detailed in the chronology drawn up by History Commons:

> August 16-September 10, 2001: FBI Fails to Brief NSC
> on Moussaoui, although this is Standard Practice
> Following the arrest of Zacarias Moussaoui, the FBI fails to brief the Counterterrorism and Security Group (CSG) chaired by counterterrorism "tsar" Richard Clarke at the National

---

78. *A Review of the FBI's Handling of Intelligence Information Related to the September 11 Attacks*, Special Report, *Chapter Four: The FBI's Investigation of Zacarias Moussaoui*, Office of the Inspector General, November 2004.

Security Council (NSC) on the case. CIA director George Tenet will later say that briefing the CSG on such an arrest is "standard practice." [Tenet, 2007, pp. 200] In July 2001, Clarke had told the FBI he wanted to be informed of anything unusual, even if a sparrow fell from a tree.[79]

It is impossible to claim that September 11 would not have taken place if Richard Clarke had been informed of this arrest, but at the very least it would have given the Minneapolis office a strong ally in securing the warrant. In summary, not only did the FBI appear to sabotage the work of its field agents, but it also did not share crucial information with the highest anti-terrorist authorities, which would prove fatal.

FBI vs. FBI—New York

On October 12, 2000, the USS *Cole* was bombed in the Yemeni port of Aden by al-Qaeda terrorists. Seventeen American soldiers were killed. Abd al-Karim al-Iryani, who was Prime Minister of Yemen at the time of the USS *Cole* attack, stated later that hijacker

Khalid Almihdhar was one of the Cole perpetrators, involved in preparations. He was in Yemen at the time and stayed after the *Cole* bombing for a while, then he left. (*The Guardian*, 10/15/2001).[80]

Nevertheless,

Almihdhar entered and left the U.S. in 2000, and entered again on July 4, 2001. (9/11 Congressional Inquiry, 7/24/03).[81]

---

79. HistoryCommons.org.
80. HistoryCommons.org.
81. *The Terror Timeline*, p. 175.

In other words, according to the Prime Minister of Yemen, nine months after participating in the USS *Cole* attack, he (quietly) entered the United States. Here is the explanation:

> The CIA and FBI have recently been showing interest in him, but have still failed to place him on a terrorist watch list. Had he been placed on a watch list by this date, he would have been stopped and possibly detained as he tried to enter the U.S. He enters on a new U.S. visa obtained in Jeddah, Saudi Arabia, on June 13, 2001. (9/11 Congressional Inquiry, 7/24/03).[82]

Astounding, considering that this was a terrorist who had killed U.S. soldiers. The mistake was fixed, but too late:

> Thanks to the request of an unnamed FBI analyst assigned to the CIAs Counter Terrorism Center, the CIA sends a cable to the State Department, INS, Customs Service, and FBI requesting that "bin Laden related individuals" Nawaf Alhazmi, Khalid Almihdhar, and two others be put on the terrorism watch list. (*Newsweek*, 6/2/02).[83]

A report was sent by the FBI's New York Field Office recommending that an investigation be launched

> "to determine if [Khalid] Almihdhar is still in the United States." The New York office tries to convince FBI headquarters to open a criminal investigation, but it is immediately turned down. The reason given is a "wall" between criminal and intelligence work-Almihdhar could not be tied to the USS *Cole* investigation without the inclusion of sensitive intelligence

---

82. *The Terror Timeline*, p. 174.
83. *The Terror Timeline*, p. 175.

information. (9/11 Congressional Inquiry, 9/20/02). So instead of a criminal case, the New York office opens an "intelligence case," excluding all the "criminal case" investigators from the search. (FBI Agent Testimony, 9/20/02).[84]

As a result of these successive "failures," Khalid Almihdhar would not be arrested until the fateful date. An FBI agent in New York ominously wrote on August 29:

> Someday someone will die. The public will not understand why we were not more effective and throwing every resource we had at certain problems.[85]

Is it necessary to comment on the FBI's responsibility?

FBI vs. FBI—Chicago

FBI agent Robert G. Wright Jr., who dealt with terrorism issues at the Chicago office, discovered evidence linking multimillionaire Saudi businessman Yassin al-Qadi to the financing of American embassy bombings in Tanzania and Kenya two months earlier. His superiors prevented him from going further, including opening a criminal investigation and making arrests:

> [...] conversations with FBI personnel indicate that he was told informally that his work was too embarrassing to the Saudis.[86]

Indeed, the Saudis should not be embarrassed in Washington. However, the case was getting stronger as Mark Flessner, a federal prosecutor involved in the investigation, pointed out after 9/11:

---

84. *The Terror Timeline*, p. 177.
85. *White House, In Shift, Backs Inquiry on 9/11*, by David Firestone and James Risen, *The New York Times*, September 21, 2002.
86. History Commons.org.

There were powers bigger than I was in the Justice Department and within the FBI that simply were not going to let [the building of a criminal case] happen. And it didn't happen.... I think there were very serious mistakes made. And I think, it perhaps cost, it cost people their lives ultimately. (ABC News, 12/19/2002).[87]

While on the subject, here is what Agent Robert Wright said three months before September 11:

Knowing what I know, I can confidently say that until the investigative responsibilities for terrorism are removed from the FBI, I will not feel safe. The FBI has proven for the past decade it cannot identify and prevent acts of terrorism against the United States and it's [*sic*] citizens at home and abroad. Even worse, there is virtually no effort on the part of the FBI's international terrorism unit to neutralize known and suspected terrorists residing within the United States.[88]

He added:

FBI management intentionally and repeatedly thwarted and obstructed my attempts to launch a more comprehensive investigation to identify and neutralize terrorists.

These are serious accusations that should have been addressed and cleared. It had been planned, but,

Supposedly, the FBI "stalled Wright's appearance before the 9/11 Commission until it was too late for him to appear before its public hearings." [US Congress, 7/24/2003;

---

87. History Commons.org.
88. https://en.wikipedia.org/wiki/Robert_Wright_Jr.

DebbieSchlussel(.com), 7/14/2004; 9/11 Commission, 7/24/2004].[89]

Robert G. Wright was nevertheless heard by the 9/11 Congressional Inquiry at the end of 2002, but neither his nor Yassin al-Qadi's names were mentioned in the final report. Neither were the investigations he conducted.

Also worth mentioning is the fact that he subsequently initiated legal proceedings against the FBI, including one concerning the publishing of his manuscript *Fatal Betrayals of the Intelligence Mission.*[90] At the time of writing *The FBI, Accomplice of 9/11*, it seems that his book has not yet been published. Yet he stated that his reason for writing it is to expose

> "the bureau's dereliction of duty in the terrorism arena," that he is "seeking a thorough review and complete 'house cleaning' to identify and fix the FBI's problems," and that "as a nation we must work together in seeking to regain the confidence level we once had in the FBI to achieve its vital mission of protecting the safety and welfare of its citizens at home and abroad." (Judicial Watch, 30/5/2002).[91]

Has trust been restored? It is up to the American people to decide, even if the answer is uncertain, especially with what happened before and after the last presidential elections.

---

89. *May 5, 2002-July 22, 2004: US Government Fails to Investigate FBI Agent Wright's Complaints*, History Commons (.org).
90. Https://fas.org/sgp/jud/wright050609.pdf.
91. History Commons.org.

Promotions and Rewards at the FBI

Colleen Rowley, among many other observers, noted that the headquarters agents who had blocked the Minnesota FBI investigation were promoted after 9/11. (*Sydney Morning Herald*, 5/28/02; *Time*, 5/21/02).[92] Indeed:

> FBI Director Mueller personally awards [X][93] with a presidential citation and cash bonus of approximately 25 percent of his salary. (*Salon*, 3/3/03).
>
> [X], head of the FBI's National Security Law Unit and the person who refused to seek a special warrant for a search of Zacarias Moussaoui's belongings before the 9/11 attacks were among nine recipients of bureau awards for "exceptional performance." The award came shortly after a 9/11 Congressional Inquiry report saying [X]'s unit gave Minneapolis FBI agents "inexcusably confused and inaccurate information" that was "patently false." (*Minneapolis Star Tribune*, 12/22/02). [X]'s unit also blocked an urgent request by FBI agents to begin searching for Khalid Almihdhar after his name was put on a watch list. Associated Press, 1/10/03).
>
> FBI Supervisory special agent [X], who removed information from the Minnesota FBI's application to get the search warrant for Moussaoui, was promoted to field supervisor. (*Salon*, 3/3/03).
>
> As Senator Charles Grassely (R) and others pointed out, not only has no one in government been fired or punished for 9/11, but several others have been promoted.[94]

---

92. *The Terror Timeline*, p. 221.
93. We will not give these names here, we are not interested in middle management but in top brass who promoted these individuals despite their repeated "failures" that contributed to the horror of 9/11 byhampering efforts to prevent it.
94. *The Terror Timeline*, pp. 555-6.

There is at least one more person to add to the list, an intelligence operations specialist in the FBI's bin Laden unit, who later became a supervisory intelligence analyst, even though she had

> repeatedly hampered the investigation of Almihdhar and Alhazmi in the summer of 2001.[95]

So why did the director "personally" hand out promotions to employees who seem to have blocked actions that could have prevented 9/11? It should be noted that these questionable promotions were not unique to the FBI and could also be found at the CIA and White House. They seem even more puzzling when reading the following pages.

---

95. *January 10, 2003: Government Employees Responsible for 9/11 Failures Are Rewarded and Promoted*, History Commons.org.

Chapter 9/4

The FBI Knew, Part 3
Officials

We have established in the two previous chapters that, contrary to what (former) directors of the FBI and others have been repeating since 2001, the possibility of al-Qaeda attacks on Washington and New York with hijacked aircraft had been conceivable and grew with increasing probability as zero-day approached. Hijackers had even been identified.

The Strange Behavior of Attorney General Ashcroft
After the attacks,

> he prevented the FBI investigating gun-purchase records to discover if any of the terrorists had bought a weapon.[96]

A strange move from the Attorney General, who should normally be in pursuit of facts. Did he consider the government version, where terrorists hijacked planes with knives and box-cutters, to be solid enough to deter investigators from pursuing other leads? Yet, when Flight 93 passenger Tom Burnett called his wife Deena, he told her that one of the terrorists had a gun. She had immediately relayed the information to emergency services, as the recording confirms.[97] Thus, the terrorists had at least one firearm and not only the bladed weapons. This is a lead the FBI should have pursued. A gun was also allegedly used on board Flight 11.[98]

---

96. *Ashcroft drawn into row over September 11*, Julian Borger, *The Guardian*, May 21, 2002.
97. *The Terror Timeline*, p. 409.
98. *The Terror Timeline*, p. 510.

Disturbing information then surfaced in the months following 9/11: John Ashcroft received a threat assessment from the FBI some time before the events and reportedly decided to stop taking commercial flights. Here is how David Ray Griffin summarized the situation in *The 9/11 Commission Report – Omissions and Distortions*:

> This story received considerable attention. 'The FBI obviously knew something was in the wind,' complained the *San Francisco Chronicle*. 'The FBI did advise Ashcroft to stay off commercial aircraft. The rest of us just had to take our chances.' CBS's Dan Rather asked, 'Why wasn't [this warning] shared with the public at large?'[99] This is surely a question that many Americans wanted answered. A reporter for the Associated Press, however, said that when Ashcroft was asked about this, he walked out of his office rather than answer.[100]
> But finally, with the report of the 9/11 Commission, we would surely find out what Ashcroft had to say about this, because the Commission, having subpoena power, could force him to submit to its questions. The issue was clearly of great importance because media reports suggested, as the *Chronicle* pointed out, that the FBI evidently had more specific information about upcoming attacks in the United States, involving commercial airliners, than it had let on. Yet if readers look up all 26 references to Ashcroft in the Commission report, they will find nothing about this matter.[101, 102]

---

99. Associated Press, May 16, 2002; *San Francisco Chronicle*, June 3, 2002; *Washington Post*, May 27, 2002.
100. Associated Press, May 16 2002.
101. Although one Commissioner did ask Ashcroft about this in a public session, this discussion was evidently one of the items not deemed important enough to include in the final report.
102. The *9/11 Commission Report, Omissions and Distortions*, Ray Griffin, Arris Books, 2005, p. 50.

How can it be that information critical in understanding the unfurling of events and the chain of responsibility was simply ignored by those responsible for uncovering the truth behind a mass murder? What did the FBI know when it gave this advice to the Attorney General Ashcroft? These questions will never be answered because a statement claiming that this warning had nothing to do with al-Qaeda and the potential hijacking of aircraft would suffice to close the case if there is no investigation. This is exactly what Mark Covallo, spokesman for the Department of Justice, announced to the *Guardian*, on May 16, 2002[103]. Although, the *Guardian* still pointed out that:

> M. Ashcroft stopped using commercial flights in July, just as the intelligence 'chatter' about a possible al-Qaida strike on US soil was getting louder.[104]

The *Guardian* journalist was not fooled; who could be fooled anyway? At the same time, Ashcroft stated

> in a July 11 speech at a domestic preparedness summit of the National Governors Association, he said, "Our No. 1 priority is the prevention of terrorist attacks."[105]

His point is one of utter seriousness. He allegedly deployed protective measures on himself as a result of information received from the FBI, but did he, the Attorney General, do the same for the American people? Would that not be the very definition of a felony? What instructions did he give to the FBI to combat this threat? What effective measures did he implement as part of the

---

103. *US asks : just what did Bush know*, Julian Borger, *The Guardian*, May 17, 2002.
104. *Ashcroft drawn into row over September 11*, Julian Borger, *The Guardian*, May 21, 2002.
105. *How Sept. 11 Changed Goals Of Justice Dept.*, by Adam Clymer, *The New York Times*, February 28, 2002.

so-called "prevention" mentioned in his speech? What agencies and administrations did he alert? Did he warn the Federal Aviation Administration (FAA) and the major airlines of any imminent danger? Is it not time to (finally) ask him these questions?

Willie Brown Too, and How Many Others?

This is all the more confusing since John Ashcroft was apparently not the only one who benefited from information of this type. For instance, the *San Francisco Chronicle* of September 12 and 14, 2001, reported that San Francisco's Mayor Willie Brown had been advised to remain cautious during his flight to New York by airport security personnel, a mere eight hours before the attacks.[106]

As Willie Brown was not auditioned by the Commission either, it is impossible to know the exact content of the alert he received and its original source.

He had later stated that it was not really an alert, just caution as is standard practice, and that he had taken his flight to New York regardless.

Similar information was published elsewhere: *Newsweek*, for example, wrote that on September 10,

> a group of top Pentagon officials suddenly canceled travel plans for the next morning, apparently because of security concerns.[107]

This is the very embodiment of inconsistent, useless news that serves only to sow confusion and fuel conspiracy theories. Who are these "senior Pentagon officials" and why add "apparently," if not to admit that this is mere journalistic speculation? Unless this was a smokescreen to protect Attorney General Ashcroft from what could be considered a felony.

---

106. *The 9/11 Commission Report, Omissions and Distortions*, p. 57.
107. *Bush: 'We're At War'*, by Evan Thomas and Mark Hosenball, *Newsweek*, 2002.

Attorney David Schippers

David Griffin reported:

> Two days after 9/11, Attorney David Schippers publicly declared that over six weeks prior to 9/11, FBI agents had given him information about attacks planned for "lower Manhattan." This information, Schippers claimed, was highly specific, including the dates, the targets, and the funding sources of the terrorists. Schippers said further that the FBI field agents told him that their investigations had been curtailed by FBI headquarters, which threatened the agents with prosecution if they went public with this information.[108]

How is it possible that agents knew details of 9/11 several weeks in advance, including the day and targets, which would have been enough to prevent it? Why did the FBI headquarters forbid them to talk publicly about it and therefore take preventive action, threatening them with prosecution if they did? The mind is hard-pressed to find any coherence behind all this; these are accusations of a major scale. Who at Headquarters could have issued such orders? And to what end?

Knowing this, how can we not suggest that the FBI was up to speed and that Headquarters—the culprits' names are yet to be revealed—stood as an accomplice of 9/11? This was not only through its failures and refusal to act on intelligence, but also what looks like sabotage against other divisions as shown previously.

David Schippers added that he had called John Ashcroft from July 15 on to warn him, but never heard back. The "he was too unimportant" card cannot be played here: Schippers was named Chief Investigative Counsel at the US House Judiciary Committee in April 1998 for the political sex scandal of President Clinton and

---

108. *The 9/11 Commission Report, Omissions and Distortions*, p. 51.

impeachment procedure. This role put him in the spotlight, but only a subordinate of Ashcroft called him back, without a follow-up.

These public declarations coming from an attorney of the United States raise questions on the FBI hierarchy's contribution to 9/11. Unsurprisingly, the Commission did not audition David Schippers. Unfortunately, his name was not even in the final *Report*. His testimony under oath would surely have revealed a number of facts and helped build public opinion, at home as well as abroad.

Three Agents and Nearly the Entire Office

Who were the agents threatened with prosecution by "their" FBI because they knew too much and were forbidden to make public statements? Having logged the suspicious behavior of their hierarchy, they notified an attorney who unfortunately had just as little success in front of the Department of Justice. When invited to the *Alex Jones Show*, he stated that some of them were ready to testify on what they know, but first needed legal protection from government.

Of course, no such protection was given to them, thus they remain unknown. As David Griffin stressed,

> We would also assume that the Commission would have been most anxious to identify and interview under oath, perhaps with lie detectors, the FBI agents who, according to Schippers, had contacted him. This should have been even more the case because Schippers' claims were confirmed by a story in a conservative magazine, *The New American*. According to this story, three FBI agents, interviewed by the author, said "that the information provided to Schippers was widely known within the Bureau before September 11th." One of them reportedly said that some of the FBI field agents — who were some of the "most experienced guys" — "predicted,

almost precisely, what happened on September 11th." This agent also reportedly said that it was widely known "all over the Bureau, how these [warnings] were ignored by Washington."[7] "Washington," of course, meant FBI headquarters, where Thomas Pickard was the Acting Director and Dale Watson the head of counterterrorism. Watson told the Commission that "he felt deeply that something was going to happen" but that "the threat information was 'nebulous'" (p. 265). Wouldn't the Commission have wanted to confront Pickard and Watson with the far-from-nebulous claims of these FBI field agents? When we check all the places in the Commission's report in which Pickard and Watson are mentioned, however, we find no indication that they were asked about these reports. We also find no discussion of any interviews with these FBI field agents.[109]

Griffin's conclusion is a bitter pill:

> The Kean-Zelikow Commission concludes that the terrorists succeeded by "exploit[ing] deep institutional failings within our government" (265). This conclusion points ahead to the Commission's recommendations, in which they propose some sweeping institutional changes. But the evidence ignored hereby the Commission is evidence of failures due not to structural flaws but to the actions-and non actions-of particular individuals: John Ashcroft, Thomas Pickard, and Dale Watson.[110]

Robert S. Mueller, named one week before 9/11, could perhaps also be added. However, what could he have done in such a

---

109. *The 9/11 Commission Report, Omissions and Distortions*, p. 51. Note 7: see footnote n° 111.
110. *The 9/11 Commission Report, Omissions and Distortions*, p. 52.

short period of time? Had he been provided access to the same information as field agents, a few days may well have proven to be enough. Could it be that the intelligence had indeed been relayed, but that he had not acted upon it, thereby not protecting the American people?

All things aside, reading the article in *The New American*[111] was highly instructive since it confirmed that all the detailed information given to David Schippers was common knowledge within the Bureau. If this were the case, why did 9/11 even take place?

If these agents accepted to talk to the journalist but only anonymously, it was because they were at risk of extreme personal and professional retaliation. We cannot really blame them when we see the usual fate, unworthy of a democracy, reserved to whistleblowers like John Kiriakou, a former CIA agent who dared reveal the torturous practices of his agency, not to mention Julian Assange's situation, and so many other courageous men and women.

Thus, it seems FBI agents were not the only ones in the know. *The Terror Timeline* (p. 65) lists two examples of teenagers warning their professor on the eve of the events:

> A fifth grader in Dallas, Texas, casually tells his teacher, "Tomorrow, World War III will begin. It will begin in the United States, and the United States will lose." The teacher reports the comment to the FBI but does not know if they act on it at the time. The student skips the next two days of school. The event may be completely coincidental, but the newspaper that reports the story also notes that two charities located in an adjacent suburb have been under investigation based on suspected fund-raising activities for Islamic terrorist organizations. (*Houston Chronicle*, 9/19/01).

111. *Did We Know What Was Coming?*, William Norman Grigg, *The New American*, March 11, 2002.

The FBI investigates and decides "no further investigation [is] warranted." (*Houston Chronicle*, 10/1/01).

A sixth-grade student of Middle Eastern descent in Jersey City, New Jersey, says something that alarms his teacher at Martin Luther King Jr. Elementary School. "Essentially, he [warns] her to stay away from lower Manhattan because something bad [is] going to happen," says Sgt. Edgar Martinez, deputy director of police services for the Jersey City Police Department. (*Insight*, 9/10/02).

Having been to New York regularly after the events ourselves, we had heard rumors of World Trade Center executives, mainly in finance, being told the day before not to come in on September 11. It is easy to understand why they preferred not to testify, should this turn out to be true.

Regardless, let us direct our attention to what Director Mueller kept repeating one year after the disaster, as we mentioned before:

To this day we have found no one in the United States except the actual hijackers who knew of the plot.[112]

He did not have to look very far: his own agency. How could he make such statements when FBI agents had uncovered the dates, targets and perpetrators, including those who were funding the operation, in advance? Was this simple incompetence, blatant lying, or both? That is for the reader to choose. In any case, there are questions for him to answer.

---

112. *The New Pearl Harbor*, p. 69.

The FBI Was Asleep

"Kill Americans"

On February 23, 1998, Osama bin Laden and Ayman al-Zawahiri co-signed a fatwa, in the name of the World Islamic Front for Jihad Against Jews and Crusaders, that declared:

> [...] As for the fighting to repulse [an enemy], it is aimed at defending sanctity and religion, and it is a duty as agreed [by the ulema]. Nothing is more sacred than belief except repulsing an enemy who is attacking religion and life.
> On that basis, and in compliance with Allah's order, we issue the following fatwa to all Muslims:
> The ruling to kill the Americans and their allies—civilians and military—is an individual duty for every Muslim who can do it in any country in which it is possible to do it, in order to liberate the al-Aqsa Mosque and the holy mosque [Mecca] from their grip, and in order for their armies to move out of all the lands of Islam, defeated and unable to threaten any Muslim. This is in accordance with the words of Almighty Allah, "and fight the pagans all together as they fight you all together," and "fight them until there is no more tumult or oppression, and there prevail justice and faith in Allah."
> [...] This is in addition to the words of Almighty Allah: "And why should ye not fight in the cause of Allah and of those who, being weak, are ill-treated (and oppressed)?—women and children, whose cry is: 'Our Lord, rescue us from this town, whose people are oppressors; and raise for us from thee one who will help!'"

O. bin Laden told the attending journalists: "You will see the results of this in a very short time."

Then both men organized an al-Qaeda congress on June 24, 1998. The "results" of their fatwa were about to come.

Could it be that the FBI, a highly specialized intelligence agency that deals with terrorism on a daily basis and had already experienced the 1993 bombing of the WTC by fanatics trained in al-Qaeda camps in Afghanistan, was not aware of this message despite the fact that it had received media coverage?

On the Ten Most Wanted List

On August 7, 1998, truck bombs exploded almost simultaneously at the United States embassies in the East African capital cities of Dar es Salaam, Tanzania and Nairobi, Kenya. 213 people were killed in Nairobi and 11 in Dar es Salam, with an estimated 4,000 and 85 wounded respectively.

The attacks brought Osama bin Laden and Ayman al-Zawahiri to the attention of the United States public for the first time. According to Wikipedia, "Bin Laden became the 456th person listed on the FBI Ten Most Wanted Fugitives list when he was added on June 7, 1999," after being indicted for murder, conspiracy and other charges in connection with the embassy bombings. A \$5 million reward was put on his head at the time (it would reach \$25 million after 9/11).

Poster from June 1999, revised in November 2001, with "a reward of up to $25 million for information leading directly to the apprehension or conviction of Osama Bin Laden. An additional $2 million is being offered through a program developed and funded by the Airline Pilots Association and the Air Transport Association."

Between Friends in Dubai

By the summer of 2001, Osama bin Laden was thus America's "most wanted" criminal, for whom it was offering a $5 million bounty. We also learn that

> the US government had supposedly tried to kill him. And yet in July, according to reports by several of Europe most respected news sources, bin Laden spent two weeks in the American hospital in Dubai (of the United Arab Emirates).[113]

---

113. Richard Labévière, *CIA Agent Allegedly Met Bin Laden in July*, Le Figaro, October 31; Anthony Sampson, *CIA Agent Alleged to Have Met bin Laden in July*, *Guardian*, November 1; Adam Sage, *Ailing bin Laden Treated for Kidney Disease,London Times*, November 1; Agence France-Presse, November 1; Radio France International, November 1; and Reuters, November 10, 2001; cited in *The Terror Timeline*, July 4-14 and July 12, 2001, and in Ahrned, 207-09; in *The New Pearl Harbor*, p. 77.

Supporting this was an article from the French newspaper *Le Figaro,* published on October 11, 2001, and written by Alexandra Richard, titled *CIA Allegedly Met bin Laden in July*[114]:

> Dubai [...] was the backdrop of a secret meeting between Osama bin Laden and the local CIA agent in July. A professional partner of the administration of the American Hospital in Dubai claims that public enemy number one stayed at this hospital between the 4th and 14th of July [2001].
>
> Coming from the Quetta airport in Pakistan, bin Laden was transferred to the hospital upon his arrival at Dubai airport. He was accompanied by his personal physician and faithful lieutenant, [...], four bodyguards, as well as a male Algerian nurse, and admitted to the American Hospital, a glass and marble building situated between the Al-Garhoud and Al-Maktoum bridges.
>
> [...] The Saudi billionaire was admitted to the well-respected urology department run by Terry Callaway, gallstone and male infertility specialist. Dr. Callaway declined to respond to our questions despite several phone calls.
>
> [...] While he was hospitalized, bin Laden received visits from many members of his family as well as prominent Saudis and Emiratis. During the hospital stay, the local CIA agent, known to many in Dubai, was seen taking the main elevator of the hospital to go to bin Laden's hospital room.
>
> A few days later, the CIA man bragged to a few friends about having visited bin Laden. Authorized sources say that on July 15th, the day after bin Laden returned to Quetta, the CIA agent was called back to headquarters.

---

114. *La CIA aurait rencontré Ben Laden en juillet*, Alexandra Richard, *Le Figaro*, October 11, 2001.

This is hardly believable, however:

> "The explosive story," comments Thompson, was "widely reported in Europe, but barely at all in the US."[115] After this story broke in November, Chossudovsky, quoting Secretary of Defense Rumsfeld's comment that finding bin Laden would be like "searching for a needle in a stack of hay," said: "But the US could have ordered his arrest and extradition in Dubai last July. But then they would not have had a pretext for waging a war."[116]

Why would a CIA representative pay a visit to a fugitive on the FBI's Ten Most Wanted list? Is it even possible that the FBI did not know that bin Laden was being cured at the American Hospital of Dubai by an American specialist? Why was he not arrested at this perfect opportunity when he had been accused of murder and conspiracy? Could it be that this would have deprived the US of an excuse to wage its "War on Terror"?

It should be noted, however, that bin Laden allegedly denied his hospitalization in Dubai in an interview on November 7, 2001. Hamid Mir published it in both his Urdu newspapers created in 1997, the *Daily Ausaf* and *Dawn*. Bin Laden's words were surprising and contradicted what he had declared at the end of September. A brief study of the pictures published of the occasion reveal that it is likely a faked photographic montage (see on next page). Therefore, the interview probably never happened and was a forgery.

---

115. *The Timeline Terror*, July 4-14, 2001, in *The New Pearl Harbor*, p. 77.
116. This statement (quoted in Ahmed, 209) occurs in Chossudovsky's Introduction to Labévière's*Le Figaro* article, November 2, 2001, www.globalresearch.ca/articles/RIC111B.htrnl.

This photo with O. bin Laden and A. al-Zawahiri, which was
allegedly taken by the journalist Hamid Mir during an exclusive
interview on November 7, 2001, is very likely forged.
Among other errors, the proportions of both faces and bodies
are not respected and the clipping against the wall
can be seen as soon as the picture is enlarged.

"Dead or Alive," Really?

In fact, what happened in Dubai became less and less surprising as
the evidence piled up. For example:

> In March of 2001, the Russian Permanent Mission at the
> United Nations secretly submitted "an unprecedentedly
> detailed report" to the UN Security Council about bin Laden
> and his whereabouts, including "a listing of all bin Laden's
> bases, his government contacts and foreign advisors"-
> enough information, they said, to kill him. But the Bush
> administration took no action. Alex Standish, the editor of

Jane's Intelligence Review, would later conclude that the attacks of 9/11 were not an intelligence failure but the result of "a political decision not to act against bin Laden."[117]

However, it can be posited that this information had arrived before September 11, when the United States did not have as many reasons to "liquidate" bin Laden. But this is without accounting for the deadly attacks on the WTC, East African embassies and USS *Cole*. In addition, the same situations occurred *after* September 11. David R. Griffin sums it up clearly:

> In addition to this story [hospital in Dubai] which suggests that the US government was less anxious to capture OBL prior to 9/11 than it said, there are also stories suggesting something similar even after 9/11, in spite of the fact that President Bush had famously spoken of wanting OBL "dead or alive." As I pointed out in *The New Pearl Harbor*, there were several articles in mainstream sources, including *Newsweek*, suggesting that the US military let OBL and his al-Qaeda forces escape on four occasions, ultimately from the Tora Bora Mountains. General Richard Myers, furthermore, said that "the goal has never been to get bin Laden."[(2)] One American official even reportedly warned of "a premature collapse of the international effort if by some lucky chance bin Laden was captured."[(3)] These actions and statements have led some critics to suspect that the US military deliberately allowed OBL and his al-Qaeda cohorts to escape, so that "the hunt for bin Laden and al-Qaeda" could be used as a pretext to achieve other US goals. An article in the *Telegraph*, in fact, said: "In retrospect, and with

---

117. *Jane's Intelligence Review*, October 5, 2001, quoted in *The Terror Timeline*, March 7, 2001, in *The New Pearl Harbor*, p. 76.

the benefit of dozens of accounts from the participants, the battle for Tora Bora looks more like a grand charade."[(4)118]

However, this begins to veer away from our FBI-focused review. Let it be added, however, that bin Laden had long interview with the Pakistani daily *Ummat,* published on September 28, 2001, i.e. seventeen days after the attacks. It would be translated and made public by the BBC World Monitoring Service on September 29, 2001. He declared:

> I have already said that I am not involved in the 11 September attacks in the United States. As a Muslim, I try my best to avoid telling a lie. I had no knowledge of these attacks, nor do I consider the killing of innocent women, children and other humans as an appreciable act. Islam strictly forbids causing harm to innocent women, children and other people. Such a practice is forbidden even in the course of a battle. [...].
> Whoever committed the act of 11 September are not the friends of the American people. I have already said that we are against the American system, not against its people, whereas in these attacks, the common American people have been killed. The United States should try to trace the perpetrators of these attacks within itself.[119]

US authorities claimed that bin Laden had gotten scared due to the punishment that awaited him, explaining the interview. The article does not support this, but we will go along with the US

---

118. The *9/11 Commission Report, Omissions and Distortions*, p. 51. Notes:

2. Department of Defense, April 6, 2002, quoted in *The New Pearl Harbor*, p. 107.

3. *Daily Mirror*, November 16, 2001.

4. *Telegraph*, February 23, 2002.

119. The original link on the BBC website is no longer available, but the interview can be read on Global Research: https://www.globalresearch.ca/interview-with-osama-bin-laden-denies-his-involvement-in-9-11/24697.

government interpretation. Notwithstanding, note that the FBI was not completely convinced of bin Laden's implication in the 9/11 attacks: he was on the FBI Ten Most Wanted Fugitives list "only" for previous attacks. Pressed for an explanation, Rex Tomb, Chief of Investigative Publicity at the FBI, answered:

> The reason why 9/11 is not mentioned on Osama bin Laden's Most Wanted page is because the FBI has no hard evidence connecting Bin Laden to 9/11.[120]

They were not alone in noticing it: one should keep in mind that the so-called proof that bin Laden orchestrated 9/11 stems from two elements:

1) The public presentation of a document on October 4, 2001, by British Prime Minister Tony Blair, entitled *Responsibility for the Terrorist Atrocities in the United States*. Listing "clear conclusions reached by the government," it began:

> "This document does not purport to provide a prosecutable case against Osama bin Laden in a court of law." This weakness was noted the next day by the BBC, which said: "There is no direct evidence in the public domain linking Osama bin Laden to the 11 September attacks. At best the evidence is circumstantial."[121]

2) So the document itself stated that it contained no solid evidence. Moving on to the second piece of evidence, the bin Laden "confession." A video tape found in Afghanistan in November 2001

---

120. Ed Haas, *FBI says, "No Hard Evidence Connecting Bin Laden to 9/11"*, Muckraker Report, June 6, 2006, (http://www.teamliberty.net/id267.html).
121. *Was America Attacked by Muslims on 9/11?*, David Ray Griffin, OpEdNews, 9/9/2008.

by agents of US intelligence services and broadcast on December 13 by the Pentagon. Briefly put, it raised so many questions that experts quickly labeled it a forgery. Therefore, it did not succeed any more than the Blair announcement in convincing the FBI to add 9/11 to the list of bin Laden's crimes.

The FBI and bin Laden's Death

According to the government version, Osama bin Laden was killed on May 2, 2011 by Navy SEAL Team Six in Abbottabad, Pakistan. Everybody saw the pictures, with Barack Obama, Joe Biden, Hillary Clinton and their teams following the operation live on a screen. But we do not see what they were really watching.

Many inconsistencies seem to prove that the mission was likely a fake. For example, a neighbor who had witnessed the events on the ground declared on Pakistani TV that only one of the three helicopters landed, but it exploded when taking off; all passengers were killed. Therefore, the corpse of bin Laden could not be thrown into the sea as it had triumphantly been announced.

Knowledge of this nature would unquestionably have required that the FBI investigate the witness, especially since others have also come forward with stories contradicting Barack Obama and Hillary Clinton.

Did the FBI refrain from investigating because it knew that bin Laden had died almost ten years earlier, three months after 9/11, in December 2001? As far-fetched as it seems, an Egyptian newspaper, *Al-Wafd*, published an obituary on December 26, 2001, pertaining to his funeral which had taken place ten days earlier at Tora Bora.[122] Also published in the *Pakistan Observer*, the news had been broken by an anonymous Taliban leader. He claimed that he had attended the funeral and seen the face of bin Laden before he was cremated.

---

122. For example, *Osama's Funeral Reported in December 2001*, Global Research, May 10, 2011.

The al-Qaeda leader had died from a pulmonary complication after his kidney problems.

Several mainstream US media reported the events, but authorities did not take it into account. Nevertheless, to everyone's surprise, a high-ranking FBI official stated in July 2002:

> The US Federal Bureau of Investigation's counter-terrorism chief, Dale Watson, says he thinks Osama bin Laden is "probably" dead.
>
> It is thought to be the first time a senior US law-enforcement official has publicly offered an opinion on whether Bin Laden, the prime suspect believed to be behind the 11 September attacks, is dead or alive.
>
> "Is (Bin Laden) alive or is he dead?" Mr. Watson said. "I am not really sure of the answer... I personally think he is probably not with us anymore, but I have no evidence to support that." The remarks, made at a law-enforcement conference in Washington on Wednesday, follow recent statements from both an Arabic newspaper editor and the chief of German foreign intelligence that Bin Laden is still alive.[123]

Thus, the FBI chief of the counterterrorism declared in July 2002 that bin Laden was "probably" dead. Such a public statement was evidently not neutral in that particular context, but it did not change the strategy and the war of the US in Afghanistan. Yet,

> British intelligence affirmed that they had been present at his burial.[124]

It is equally worth mentioning that in January 2002, the President

---

123. *Bin Laden 'probably' dead*, BBC News World Edition, 07/18/2002.
124. *Une commission d'enquête sur la mort des soldats qui auraient tué Ben Laden*, Réseau Voltaire, July 27, 2013.

of Pakistan General Pervez Musharraf, also declared that bin Laden was dead, followed by Israeli intelligence. The CIA even closed its unit in charge to hunt down bin Laden and his lieutenants at the end of 2005. Nevertheless,

> "The efforts to find Osama bin Laden are as strong as ever," said Jennifer Millerwise Dyck, a CIA. spokeswoman.[125]

Undoubtedly so.

Similar announcements of bin Laden's death arose throughout 2002 but, for the Obama administration, and therefore the US, he only died on May 2, 2011, almost ten years after his "first" death. The FBI did not investigate his "second demise."

Bin Laden Brings Bad Luck

Under the title *November 28, 2001: Bin Laden Reportedly Escapes Tora Bora by Helicopter*, *The Terror Timeline* relates the following story:

> A U.S. Special Forces soldier stationed in Fayetteville, North Carolina later (anonymously) claims that the U.S. has bin Laden pinned in a certain Tora Bora cave on this day, but fails to act. Special Forces soldiers allegedly sit by waiting for orders and watch two helicopters fly into the area where bin Laden is believed to be, load up passengers, and fly toward Pakistan. No other soldiers have come forward to corroborate the story, but bin Laden is widely believed to have been in the Tora Bora area at the time. (*Fayetteville Observer*, 8/2/02).
>
> However, other reports indicate that bin Laden may have left the Tora Bora region by this time. *Newsweek* separately reports

---

125. *C.I.A. Closes Unit Focused on Capture of bin Laden*, by Mark Mazzetti, *The New York Times*, July 4, 2006.

that many locals "claim that mysterious black helicopters swept in, flying low over the mountains at night, and scooped up al-Qaeda's top leaders." (*Newsweek*, 8/11/02).

Perhaps coincidentally, on the same day this story is reported, months after the fact, the media also will report a recent spate of strange deaths at the same military base in Fayetteville. Five soldiers and their wives all die since June 2002 in apparent murder-suicides. At least three were Special Forces soldiers recently returned from Afghanistan. (*Independent*, 8/2/02). [126]

Did these U.S. Special Forces soldiers of Fayetteville see bin Laden's helicopter rescue from his Tora Bora cave, then return and "commit suicide" with their wives? What does the FBI think of this?

Bin Laden Brings Bad Luck, Part 2

If we stick to the government version, it was SEAL Team Six that killed bin Laden on May 2, 2011. Later that year, on August 6, a rocket launched by the Taliban in Afghanistan hit a US army helicopter in flight, killing 38 military personnel on-board. 15 of those casualties were members of that very same SEAL Team Six. They will never be able to testify as to what really happened in Abbottabad.

Foreshadowing Domain Names

This part, lighter in nature than the latter, raises new questions about the role that the FBI played before and after 9/11. Indeed, eight days later, on September 19, 2001, an article by Jeff Johnson titled *Internet Domain Names May Have Warned of Attacks* opens:

> The terrorists who planned and executed the September 11 attack on America may have registered as many as 20 Internet

---

126. *The Terror Timeline*, p. 478.

domain names, or web addresses, that experts believe should have warned authorities of a possible assault on the World Trade Center in New York City.[127]

An article with a list of domain names was published and completed the day after, amounting to seventeen names in total:[128]

attackamerica.com	terrorattack2001.com
attackonamerica.com	towerofhorror.com
attackontwintowers.com	tradetowerstrike.com
august11horror.com	worldtradecenter929.com
august11terror.com	worldtradecenterbombs.com
horrorinamerica.com	worldtradetowerattack.com
horrorinnewyork.com	worldtradetowerstrike.com
nycterroriststrike.com	wterroristattack2001.com
pearlharborinmanhattan.com	

Domain names such as attackonamerica.com, attackontwintowers.com, terrorattack2001.com, or worldtradecenterbombs.com contain, in retrospect, paramount clues. Therefore, Neil Livingstone, head of Global Options LLC, a Washington D.C.-based counter-terrorism and investigation company, did not hesitate to declare:

---

127. Internet Domain Names May Have Warned of Attack, Jeff Johnson, CNS-News.com Congressional Bureau Chief, September 19, 2001.
128. *Investigators Can Access Internet Domain Data,* Jeff Johnson, CNSNews.com Congressional Bureau Chief, September 19, 2001. All next quotations stem from one of the two articles of Jeff Johnson.

> It's unbelievable that they (the registration company) would register these domain names, probably without any comment to the FBI.

This statement may seem exaggerated given the number of registered domain names today; more than 300 million counting only top-level domains (.com, .net, .org, etc.[129]). Of course, this figure was much lower in the year 2000, which is when these seventeen domains seem to have been bought. Since Verisign data does not go back beyond 2010, we studied the trend of website creation between 1999 and 2000: it increased from 3,177,453 to 17,087,182, thus +438%.[130] If the number of domain names registered followed the same trend during the period, it would have proven difficult to control everything manually.

An unlikely collection of circumstances is the only situation that could have triggered a warning related to the list of about twenty suspicious domains otherwise drowned in the masses.

Neil Livingstone then added:

> If they did make a comment to the FBI, it's unbelievable that the FBI didn't react to it.

In fact,

> A spokeswoman in the FBI press office would only say that the agency will not comment on its investigation into the attacks.

We do not know if the FBI attempted to identify the mysterious buyers of these domain names. If it did not, it would be mystifying. If it did, why not publish the results? Even if it led to a dead end, it would at least have allowed to close the case. However, this

---

129. Source: Verisign, *The Verisign Domain Name Industry Brief, Q1 2018*.
130. Source: Total number of Websites, internetlivestats.com.

investigation logically gave precious information, such as the names and coordinates of these strange buyers, including the credit cards used for subscription payment. Other useful information could also have been collected since four names on the list were bought again after 9/11, as reported by Jeff Johnson: attackamerica. com, attackonamerica.com, attackontwintowers.com and worldtradecenterbombs.com.

We checked, and one of them is still registered, although it does not seem active, as no website appears for this domain name:

Two other listed domains are for sale, for example:

Let us hope they will never be bought.

The FBI Silenced

The Odigo Case, a Message that Saved Lives

In *9/11 The Big Lie* (pp. 36-37), Thierry Meyssan stresses that the number of victims in New York is far lower than it should have been, which leads him to believe that:

> Despite appearances, the attacks did not aim to produce the maximum possible deaths. On the contrary, prior intervention was required to ensure that numerous persons, at least those working on the top floors, were absent from their offices at the critical hour.

This observation refers to an article published on September 26, 2001, by *Haaretz*, one of the leading Israeli newspapers:

> Odigo, the instant messaging service, says that two of its workers received messages two hours before the Twin Towers attack on September 11 predicting the attack would happen, and the company has been cooperating with Israeli and American law enforcement, including the FBI, in trying to find the original sender of the message predicting the attack.[131]

Based in Herzliyya and New York, two blocks from the WTC, Odigo was one of the largest instant messaging companies at the time. The information was taken up and followed up on two days later by the *Washington Post*, which concluded:

---

131. *Odigo Says Workers Were Warned of Attack*, Yuval Dror, *Haaretz*, 09.26.2001.

> Citing a pending investigation by law enforcement, the company declined to reveal the exact contents of the message or to identify the sender.[132]

Indeed, the FBI asked Odigo not to reveal anything else on the subject and was given the sender's name for identification.[133] As far as we know, no further mention was made of the Odigo messages. This comes as no surprise with the FBI since the government version was being called into question. It would nevertheless have been useful to know the contents of the message and the ID of the sender, as Andreas von Bülow remarked:

> If this had been the case, the aircraft intended to be hijacked would not even have been in the air at the time the message was received![134]

It is unfortunate that no information was provided on the alerts, because, as Thierry Meyssan points out, this would also reveal

> the measures taken to limit the number of persons in the towers that day. [...] Warnings of various types could have been addressed to the occupants of North Tower, even if all of them were not taken seriously in the same way.[135]

Instead, just after the FBI's intervention, it was stated that the messages did not refer to the WTC. Should we take their word for it? Regardless, they probably did save lives. Unsurprisingly though, the Commission did not mention Odigo in the *Report*. Indeed, confirmation of the messages' contents and sender would certainly

---

132. *Instant Messages to Israel Warned of WTC Attack*, The Washington Post, September 28, 2001.
133. *The Terror Timeline*, p. 308.
134. *Die CIA und der 11. September*, Andreas von Bülow, Piper Verlag, 2003, p. 129.
135. *9/11 The Big Lie*, pp. 37 and 86.

have been too risky. In other words, it would constitute one more piece of evidence that people had known exactly what was going to happen, thus reducing the government version of the conspiracy to nothing more but a (big) lie. As for Director Mueller's recurring statement that only the terrorists knew of the incoming attack; it seems increasingly devoid of any truth.

Odigo was bought by Comverse Technology the following year, in 2002, for about $20 million, before being shut down in 2004. And so, the Odigo case was closed, its only traces now lurking deep within the FBI archives.

A Fabricated List of Hijackers?

This delicate but crucial section on the identification of the 9/11 perpetrators will begin with the introduction of Jay Kolar's study, *What We Know About the Alleged 9/11 Hijackers*:

> FBI Director Mueller has admitted his case against 19 FBI-named hijackers would never stand up in a court of law.[136] Despite his admission, however, the FBI has refused to alter its list. And only one month after the FBI began to investigate the alleged hijackers, President Bush himself called off their investigation on the pretext that manpower was needed to fight the anthrax threat. After that threat dissipated, the hijacking investigation itself had been hijacked: the FBI never returned to complete it. And the FBI never released the original 9-11 airline flight manifests after it had quickly confiscated them.[137]

---

136. We do not know the circumstances of this statement and its precise words, but it sounds so accurate according to what follows, that we kept it.
137. *What We Know About the Alleged 9/11 Hijackers*, Jay Kolar, Emerald Group Publishing, 2006.

The anthrax story will be addressed in next chapter because it was a critical element in the 9/11 Operation, as much as the four planes and Muslim hijackers. On this crucial question, many authors, among them Thierry Meyssan and David Griffin, stress that the passenger manifests initially published by airlines did not contain Arabic names:

> Another problem in the official account is that, although we are told that four or five of the alleged hijackers were on each of the four flights, no proof of this claim has been provided. The story, of course, is that they did not force their way onto the planes but were regular, ticketed passengers. If so, their names should be on the flight manifests. But the flight manifests that have been released contain neither the names of the alleged hijackers nor any other Arab names.[(29)138]

In the above text, note 29 refers to the internet links published by CNN with a list for each flight. As they are no longer active, we were unable to check these manifests. However, it is important to note that at least two employees, Ed Freni, Director of aviation operations at Boston's Logan Airport, and Robert Bonner, head of Customs and Border Protection, declared that they had received the passenger lists that morning and that there had indeed been Arabic names. Thierry Meyssan notes, however:

> If one refers to the list of victims published by the airline companies on September 13, one is surprised not to see among them the names of the hijackers. It would seem that the criminals were removed in order to leave only "innocent victims" and crew members.[139]

---

138. *9/11: The Myth and the Reality*, David Ray Griffin, lecture delivered on March 30, 2006, at Grand Lake Theater in Oakland for Progressive Democrats of the East Bay, http://911truth.org.
139. *9/11 The Big Lie*, pp. 55-56.

This is also the explanation that would be given later: it was not the passenger lists that were published, but the lists of innocent victims. Such a statement raises questions about the methodology of the FBI: how did they distinguish between terrorists and victims in under two days without a formal claim? Were terrorists chosen according to how their names sounded? Thierry Meyssan pursues:

> If one refers to the press releases issued by the airlines on September 11 [circulated by the Associated Press agency], one notes that flight 11 transported 81 passengers, flight 175 carried 56 passengers, flight 77 transported 58 passengers and flight 93 had 38 passengers.

These figures give the following table:

	Passengers Numbers		
	On 9/11	On 9/13	
AA11	78	81	North Tower
UA175	46	56	South Tower
AA77	51	58	Pentagon
UA93	36	38	Pennsylvania

> Note: According to its dedicated Wikipedia page, United Airlines Flight 93 carried 37 passengers, one less than in the table.

In comparing the two columns, Thierry Meyssan comes to the following conclusion:

> It is thus physically impossible that Flight 11 could have transported more than three terrorists and Flight 93 more

than two. The absence of the names of the hijackers on the passenger lists therefore does not mean they were withdrawn in order to remain "politically correct", but simply they were not to be found among the rest. Goodbye to the identification of Mohammed Atta by a steward thanks to the seat number, 8D.

****

To sum things up, the FBI invented a list of hijackers from which it drew an identikit portrait of the enemies of the West. We are asked to believe that these hijackers were Arab Islamic militants who were acting as kamikazes. The domestic American leads were dismissed. In reality, we know nothing, neither the identity of the "terrorists" nor their operational method. All hypotheses remain open. As in all criminal affairs, the first question that should be asked is, "Who profits from the crime?"

A few weeks after *9/11 The Big Lie* was published,

The New Yorker reports that a senior FBI official acknowledges there has been "no breakthrough" in establishing how the 9/11 suicide teams were organized and how they operated. Additionally, none of the thousands of pages of documents and computer hard drives captured in Afghanistan has enabled investigators to broaden their understanding of how the attack occurred, or even to bring an indictment of a conspirator. (*New Yorker*, 5/27/02).[140]

Has any progress been made eighteen years later? Unfortunately, one can no longer consult the initial passenger manifests, thereby making it impossible to know whether the terrorists were really registered on them. This would have been especially interesting

---

140. *The Terror Timeline*, p. 512.

since officials claim to have seen Arabic names on the lists they received. The fact that some of the hijackers who had supposedly died in the four attacks were alive and well in their home countries would also not be given further attention.

All of the above questions the FBI protocol, and it is not the only point of concern:

> On September 11, the FBI asked the airlines not to communicate with the press. Yet, their testimony would help elucidate both the reasons why the planes were not filled, and why the hijackers were not on the passenger flights.[141]

The hushing-up was not limited to airlines:

> From the moment flight AA77 disappeared, officially at around 8:55 am, all information about it comes exclusively from military sources. The FBI even ordered the civil aviation authorities not to divulge any information concerning this plane. "Details about who was on Flight 77, when it took off and what happened on board were tightly held by airline, airport and security officials last night," the *Washington Post* explained." All said that the FBI had asked them not to divulge details.[142]

Why prohibit airline communication with the media if everything was clear and without any doubt on passenger lists? Even on this, a point where there should be no ambiguity, there are yet again grey areas with no rational explanation—for more on this subject read Gerard Holmgren's comparative study on Flight 11 titled *Media*

---

141. *9/11 The Big Lie*, p. 85.
142. *On Flight 77: Our Plane Is Being Hijacked, Washington Post*, September 12, 2001, in *Pentagate*, p. 92.

published fake passenger lists for American Airlines Flight 11.[143] He introduces his work with the following paragraph:

> Any crime of this magnitude, is—or should be—subject to rigorous examination by investigative and law enforcement authorities, such as the FBI. In any crime involving the illegal use of a plane, it is obvious that one of the first investigative steps taken by such authorities is to find out who was on the plane.
>
> This is not a difficult thing to do. Airlines keep well organized records of everybody on any particular flight. The apparent ID of anyone on that flight—regardless of whether they used a true or false ID—should be immediately available to authorities. Unless authorities decide that disclosure of such information may jeopardize the investigation, it should also be easily available to the media. It should be as simple as an exchange of faxes or emails between the media and either the airline involved or one of the relevant authorities to which the airline has released the information. Or possibly printed copies handed out at a press conference.

However, it is not how things played out. The story of these manifests is littered with inconsistencies and anomalies. Of course, this did not escape David Griffin's watchful eye, who writes in his article *Was America Attacked by Muslims on 9/11?* in question 8. *Were the Names of the "Hijackers" on the Passenger Manifests?*[144]:

> If the alleged hijackers purchased tickets and boarded the flights, their names would have been on the manifests for

143. *Media published fake passenger lists for American Airlines Flight 11*, Gerard Holmgren, May 16, 2004, http://portland.indymedia.org/en/2004/05/288505.shtml.
144. *Was America Attacked by Muslims on 9/11?*, David Ray Griffin, September 9, 2008, https://www.opednews.com/articles/Was-America-Attacked-by-Mu-by-David-Ray-Griffin-080909-536.html

these flights. And we were told that they were. According to counterterrorism coordinator Richard Clarke, the FBI told him at about 10:00 that morning that it recognized the names of some al-Qaeda operatives on passenger manifests it had received from the airlines.[77] As to how the FBI itself acquired its list, Robert Bonner, the head of Customs and Border Protection, said to the 9/11 Commission in 2004:

"On the morning of 9/11, through an evaluation of data related to the passenger manifest for the four terrorist hijacked aircraft, Customs Office of Intelligence was able to identify the likely terrorist hijackers. Within 45 minutes of the attacks, Customs forwarded the passenger lists with the names of the victims and 19 probable hijackers to the FBI and the intelligence community."[78] [145]

The above statement is partially contradicted by Richard Clarke in his book *Against All Enemies: Inside America's War on Terror* (pp. 13-14), who says he was told in private by Dale Watson, head of the FBI's Counterterrorism Division:

We got the passenger manifests from the airlines. We recognize some names, Dick. They're al-Qaeda." Clarke asks, "How the f_ck did they get on board then?" Watson replies: "Hey, don't shoot the messenger, friend. CIA forgot to tell us about them.[146]

---

145. Notes 77 and 78 of the article:
77. Richard A. Clarke, *Against All Enemies*: *Inside America's War on Terror* (New York: Free Press, 2004), 13.
78. "Statement of Robert C. Bonner to the National Commission on Terrorist Attacks upon the United States," 26 January 2004 (http://www.9-11commission. gov/hearings/hearing7/witness_bonner.htm).
146. HistoryCommons.org

Thus, the FBI received the passenger manifests directly from airlines, which seems to be the most logical process. Robert Bonner's statement is nevertheless problematic, all the more as he confirmed it again two weeks later:

> "And by looking at the Arab names and their seat locations, ticket purchases and other passenger information, it didn't take a lot to do a rudimentary link analysis. Customs officers were able to ID 19 probable hijackers within 45 minutes. I saw the sheet by 11 a.m. And that analysis did indeed correctly identify the terrorists." [*New York Observer*, 2/15/2004].[147]

Strange, since the initial FBI list only had eighteen names, with several being changed as the days went by, mainly because at least five "terrorists" were alive in their home countries. So, how could the Customs Office of Intelligence confirm the exact list in less an hour, whereas the FBI could not, even after using a primary and reliable source of information that was both airlines? Did Robert Bonner lie in order to subsequently confirm the government conspiracy theory? David Griffin, who details in his article a significant number of inconsistencies about the published lists, comes to the following conclusion:

> In sum, no credible evidence that al-Qaeda operatives were on the flights is provided by the passenger manifests.

He also points out:

> These replacements to the initial list also undermine the claim that Amy Sweeney, by giving the seat numbers of three of the hijackers to Michael Woodward of American Airlines, allowed him to identify Atta and two others [Flight 11]. This second

---

147. HistoryCommons.org.

claim is impossible because the two others were Abdul al-Omari and Satam al-Suqami,[82] and they were replacements for two men on the original list—who, like Adnan Bukhari, turned up alive after 9/11.[83] Woodward could not possibly have identified men who were not added to the list until several days later.[84]

For all these reasons, the claim that the names of the 19 alleged hijackers were on the airlines' passenger manifests must be considered false.[148]

Lists with the names of the hijackers would later be published and often presented as the originals. Such claims were, however, impossible. For example, the name of Hani Hanjour was written on the Flight 77 manifest, but only after it had been added by the FBI later. The *Washington Post* picked up on this anomaly and is quoted by David Griffin.[149] Despite this, these "original" documents will be used in the Moussaoui trial:

> What is striking about official reports is that it took several days to confirm the total number of hijackers. There is no explanation why someone named "Mosear Caned" was placed on a list of Hijackers and why he was replaced by Hani Hanjour. The explanation given for Hanjour's absence from the

---

148. Notes 82 to 84 of the article:

82. Gail Sheehy, "Stewardess ID'd Hijackers Early, Transcripts Show," *New York Observer*, 15 February 2004 (http://www.observer.com/node/48805).

83. Satam al-Suqami replaced a man named Amer Kamfar, and Abdulaziz al-Omari replaced a man with a similar name, Abdulrahman al-Omari; see Kolar, "What We Now Know," 12-15.

84. Another problem with the claim that Woodward had identified these three men is that the seat numbers reportedly used to identify Atta and al-Omari (see Gail Sheehy, "Stewardess ID'd Hijackers Early") did not match the numbers of the seats assigned to these two men (9/11CR 2).

149. *Was America Attacked by Muslims on 9/11?*. Note 91: *Four Planes, Four Co-ordinated Teams*, *Washington Post*, September 16, 2001.

initial list of suspects was that Hanjour "was not on the flight manifest."[42] This cannot be the case however, because Hanjour's name appears on the flight manifests provided in the Moussaoui trial. This is a clear contradiction that must be explained.[150]

Fortunately, we can always rely on the FBI for a solid explanation.

What added even further to the confusion was the fact that some passengers did not feature on the initial lists either, as was the case for Mark Bingham from Flight 93.[151] We have also compared the passenger manifests published by several media such *USA Today*, the *Boston Globe*, the *Guardian* and even the neverforget911.org website. We note, for instance on Flight AA11, that there were differences between their lists. Why did the FBI let such confusion spread? These are victims and their families. Questions of confidentiality and privacy could not be argued as the names were hastily published.

What is also disturbing are the repeated statements made by Robert Bonner claiming that the Customs Office of Intelligence had correctly identified the nineteen hijackers in forty-five minutes. How was the FBI incapable of doing so, despite having received the list from Customs? The cardinal manifest mystery remains unsolved and, therefore, we still do not know who was on board. Indeed, neither the government nor FBI ever published the authentic lists. Why? Was this an elaborate attempt at keeping the government-sanctioned version of 9/11 afloat?

---

150. Note 42: *Washington Post, Four Planes, Four Coordinated Teams*, http://www. washingtonpost.com, September 16, 2001, quoted in *9/11 Misinformation: Flight 'Passenger Lists' Show 'No Hijacker Names'*, by Arabesque, September 3, 2008, http://arabesque911.blogspot.com/2008/08/911-misinformation-flight-passenger. html.
151. http://911myths.com/html/the_passengers.html

No Manifests, and the List Goes on

Passenger lists are always carefully drawn up by airlines for security and insurance purposes. Boarding passes are equally important as they confirm the presence and identity of who is really on board. Therefore, at the time of the boarding, the staff keep the stub of every boarding pass, each with their holder's name. Yet, as noticed by Elias Davidsson in his study *There is no evidence that Muslims hijacked planes on 9/11* dated 10 January 2008:

> The 9/11 Commission Staff report,[57] which mentions specifically that Mohammed Atta received a "boarding pass" at Portland airport, does not mention boarding passes in connection with flights AA11, AA77, UA175 and UA93 as if such documents did not exist. In footnote 62 to Chapter I of its Final Report, the 9/11 Commission mentions to have received "copies of electronic boarding passes for United 93" and in footnote 74 "copies of boarding passes for United 93." None of these documents were released.[152]

Why not release the documents for any of the four flights? Once again, is there anything to hide?

Equally surprising to Elias Davidsson is the fact that:

> Normally there would have been at least eight airline employees—two for each flight—tearing off the stubs of passengers' boarding cards and observing the boarding of the four aircraft at the departure gates. Under the circumstances of 9/11, one would have expected to read international media interviews with these airline employees, or at least some of them, under headlines such as "I was the last person to see the passengers alive." Yet no such interview is known to have

---

152. Note 57: *Staff Report*, supra n° 3, quoted in *There is no evidence that Muslims hijacked planes on 9/11* Elias Davidsson, 1/10/2008, p. 8.

taken place. The 9/11 Commission does not mention the existence of any deposition or testimony by airline personnel that witnessed the boarding of the aircraft. Their identities and the role they played on 9/11 remain a secret.

Consequently, Elias Davidsson requested an interview with the American Airlines employees who last saw the passengers of AA77. But the airline responded that their identities could not be revealed for privacy reasons. Was this the FBI's will?

No Witnesses to Boarding?

The *Report* of the 9/11 Commission explains that, for "additional security scrutiny," ten of the nineteen suspects had been selected by the automated CAPPS system at the airports. Nine of them were on the American Airlines flights.[153] Elias Davidsson states:

> Yet no one of those who handled the selectees, or any of the numerous airline or airport security employees interviewed by the FBI or the Federal Aviation Administration (FAA) on or after 9/11 is known to have seen the suspects.
> As for flights AA11 and UA175, which reportedly left from Logan Airport, Boston, the 9/11 Commission found that "[n] one of the [security] checkpoint supervisors recalled the hijackers or reported anything suspicious regarding their screening."[40]
> As for flight AA77, which reportedly left from Dulles Airport, Washington, D.C., the 9/11 Commission wrote that "[w]hen the local civil aviation security office of the FAA later investigated these security screening operations, the screeners recalled nothing out of the ordinary. They could not recall that any of the passengers they screened were CAPPS selectees."[41]

153. *Final Report*, 9/11 Commission, Chapter 1, note 2, p. 451.

As for flight UA93, which reportedly left from New Jersey International Airport, the 9/11 Commission indicated that the "FAA interviewed the screeners later; none recalled anything unusual or suspicious."[42] According to an undated FBI report, the 'FBI collected 14 knives or portions of knives at the Flight 93 crash site.'[43] Yet no screener is known to have mentioned coming across a single knife that morning.[44] To sum this paragraph, no airport security employee has testified to have actually seen any of the alleged hijackers.[154]

There is, however, at least one testimony referring to a hijacker:

[...] a baggage handler for Globe Aviation and American Airlines has told the FBI that one of the hijackers—believed to be either Wail or Waleed Alshehri—was carrying one wooden crutch under his arm when he boarded Flight 11. [...]. (Boston Globe, 10/10/2001).

This does not dispel how strange the absence of other testimonies is, especially since ten terrorists had been selected by the CAPPS system and thus underwent additional security checks of their luggage. Under what circumstances did boarding take place? This will be explored further in the chapter *9/11 The FBI Lies*.

---

154. *There is no evidence that Muslims hijacked planes on 9/11,* Elias Davidsson, 10/1/2008, p. 6. Notes 40 to 44 : 40 Ibid. Chapter I, p. 2. In support of this statement, the Commission refers to interviews with six named individuals.
41 Ibid. Chapter I, p. 3. In support of this statement, the Commission refers to an interview made on April 12, 2004 with Tim Jackson, a person whose role is not indicated.
42 Ibid. Chapter I. p. 4. In support of this statement, the Commission refers to an unreleased FAA report, "United Airlines Flight 93, September 11, 2001, Executive Report," of Jan. 30, 2002.
43 Ibid. Note 82, p. 457
44 Staff Statement No. 3 to the 9/11 Commission made at the 7th Public Hearing, 26-27 January 2004, pp. 9-10.

Spotted by CCTV?

Even if nobody could recall seeing the terrorists, they must have been caught on CCTV. In fact,

> Until 2004, the only video available to the public showing the alleged hijackers at any airport was a clip from a security camera at the Portland, Maine airport showing Mohammed Atta and Abdulaziz al-Omari going through security.[1] The public has not been treated to any video showing any of the alleged hijackers at Boston Logan Airport, the origin of Flights 11 and 175, or Newark Airport, the origin of Flight 93.[155]

Indeed, Boston's Logan Airport was not equipped with such security systems at the time, therefore footage of AA11 and UA175 was lacking. Although the Commission wrote in its final report that the Newark airport did not have internal CCTV[156], the article reports that

> According to Michael Taylor, president of American International Security Corp, the Newark airport does have video cameras in its departure lounges. So does Dulles International Airport. However, the FBI has refused to release any video from these airports that might prove that the alleged hijackers boarded the flights.

No further comment is needed. Consequently, the video taken in Portland is the only one broadcast long after the events, leading Jay Kolar to point out:

---

155. *Airport Video – No Video Shows Hijackers Boarding Targeted Flights,* http://911research.wtc7.net/planes/evidence/airportvideo.html.
Note (1): *Company Helps 9/11 Probe After Losing One of Its Own*, Boston.com.
156. *The 9/11 Commission Report*, p. 4.

Through this footage, the FBI was able to identify Atta as the terrorist ringleader, although it was never explained how the FBI could identify him so quickly. However, the Portland video does not count as proof that Atta and al-Omari hijacked the plane that crashed, since this video only depicts them boarding a connecting flight.[157]

Finally:

In 2004, *USA Today* released images from a "surveillance video from Washington Dulles International Airport the morning of Sept. 11, 2001" which showed "four of the five hijackers being pulled aside to undergo additional scrutiny after setting off metal detectors."[31] The video was only obtained after a lawsuit from the "Motley Rice law firm... representing some survivors' families who are suing the airlines and security industry over their actions in the Sept. 11 attacks."[32] [...] Unusually, the video does not have a time stamp on it. However, the released video has clearly been edited since the film is slowed down and zoomed in at certain parts to emphasize the alleged hijackers. As well, the footage appears to be a combination of two different camera shots because there is more than one camera angle.[34][158]

---

157. *What We Know About the Alleged 9/11 Hijackers*, Jay Kolar, Emerald Group Publishing, 2006, p. 6.
158. *9/11 Misinformation: Flight 'Passenger Lists' Show 'No Hijacker Names'*, by Arabesque- September 3, 2008. Notes (31) to (34):
(31) The Associated Press, Video shows 9/11 hijackers' security check , http://www.usatoday.com/ , July 21, 2004
(32) The Associated Press, Video shows 9/11 hijackers' security check
(33) Bill Hutchinson, *Shocking video of hijackers set off metal detectors*, http://www.nydailynews.com/, July 22, 2004
(34) Court TV Online, *9/11 Hijackers Screened Before Flight*, http://www.courttv.com/(this link does not work anymore).

Elias Davidsson sums up Jay Kolar's study of the video as follows:

> His conclusion is that someone deliberately decided to film certain persons passing a security checkpoint at a certain time in order to produce "evidence." The released recording does not show any passengers pass through the security checkpoint. Aside from the dubious source of this recording, it does not show who boarded the aircraft but only a few individuals who passed some security checkpoint at an unknown time.[159]

David Griffin also concludes:

> [...] therefore, this video contains no evidence that it was taken at Dulles on September 11.
> [...] In sum: Video proof that the named hijackers checked into airports on 9/11 is nonexistent.[160]

Where Are the Hijackers?

After reading these facts and conclusions, if some (or all) hijackers were not onboard, then where were they? Apart from the listed names still alive after the events and gradually replaced by the FBI, it is difficult to know.

Even after all these years, there is still little clarity surrounding the who and how. One of the most striking cases is Mohamed Atta, considered as one of the ring leaders of Operation 9/11 and the pilot for Flight AA11. A video shows him at Portland airport on the morning of September 11, but not at Boston. No evidence (video, boarding pass, testimony, etc.) was brought forward on what he

---

159. *There is no evidence that Muslims hijacked planes on 9/11*, Elias Davidsson,10 January 2008, p. 2.
160. *Was America Attacked by Muslims on 9/11?, 7.Were al-Qaeda Operatives Captured on Airport Security Videos?*.

did at Boston until the crash of the plane he allegedly hijacked and piloted.

The circumstances behind Atta's luggage and round trips between Portland and Boston are also intriguing—the story is now too long to explain since it was rewritten by the FBI as inconsistencies appeared in successive versions. For a detailed insight, read *6. Did the Information in Atta's Luggage Prove the Responsibility of al-Qaeda Operatives?*, from David Griffin's article *Was America Attacked by Muslims on 9/11?*, or the study of Jay Kolar, who sums up the case as follows:

> Now, it is uniformly reported that Atta and Abdul Aziz al-Omari rented the Nissan Altima at Boston Logan, drove to Portland, left the Nissan there, and took the connecting flight back to Boston. Add to this latter inexplicable mystery the fact that *another* car rented allegedly by Atta, a white Mitsubishi, was abandoned at Boston Logan. When their destination was Boston, why would Atta and al-Omari rent one car in Boston and leave it at the Boston airport, then rent another car in Boston and leave it at the Portland, Maine, airport, and take a flight back to Boston? The whole story makes no sense. From the point of view of the alleged Arab perpetrators, why would they go out of their way to rely on a connecting flight into Boston in the first place when they risked the danger of missing their connection? What this story does suggest, however, is that just as the story about the two Bukharis renting the Nissan was found to be an impossibility—one of them being dead[161]—and as such a fabrication by the FBI, so also was the substitute story of Atta and al-Omari a fabrication and a myth.[162]

---

161. Ameer Bukhari was killed in Florida exactly a year before the 9/11 attacks, on September 11, 2000, in a midair collision between his Piper and another one.
162. *What We Know About the Alleged 9/11 Hijackers*, Jay Kolar, p. 17.

Let us address the mystery of Atta's luggage, summarized by David Griffin as follows:

> I come now to the evidence that is said to provide the strongest proof that the planes had been hijacked by Mohamed Atta and other members of al-Qaeda. This evidence was reportedly found in two pieces of Atta's luggage that were discovered inside the Boston airport after the attacks. The luggage was there, we were told, because although Atta was already in Boston on September 10, he and another al-Qaeda operative, Abdul al-Omari, rented a blue Nissan and drove up to Portland, Maine, and stayed overnight. They caught a commuter flight back to Boston early the next morning in time to get on American Flight 11, but Atta's luggage did not make it.[163]

An hour-long layover should have been enough for a baggage transfer. Nevertheless, it could have gotten lost somewhere along the way. No explanation has been offered by the FBI for whom this was an unbelievable stroke of luck. To the Bureau and the government, the pieces of evidence found in the luggage are considered as the ultimate proof that al-Qaeda, and thus Osama bin Laden, was behind the 9/11 attacks.

> This luggage, according to the FBI affidavit signed by James Lechner, contained much incriminating material, including a handheld flight computer, flight simulator manuals, two videotapes about Boeing aircraft, a slide-rule flight calculator, a copy of the Koran, and Atta's last will and testament.[164]

---

163. *Was America Attacked by Muslims on 9/11?*,6. *Did the Information in Atta's Luggage Prove the Responsibility of al-Qaeda Operatives?*, David Griffin.
164. *Was America Attacked by Muslims on 9/11?*,6. *Did the Information in Atta's Luggage Prove the Responsibility of al-Qaeda Operatives?*, David Griffin.

As many observers and journalists note, however, there were bizarre decisions made by Atta surrounding his luggage:

1. bothering oneself with luggage to commit a suicide-attack;

2. putting the handheld flight computer and slide-rule calculator in the hold when they could have been useful onboard;

3. bringing a will onboard a plane knowing it will inevitably be destroyed.

Furthermore, do these articles prove beyond all doubt what Atta has been accused of? A five-page document handwritten in Arabic was conveniently added, which will be discussed in chapter *9/9 The FBI Forged False Evidence?*

Consequently, the story of Atta's luggage and round trips between Portland and Boston led many authors to conclude that it was staged by the FBI. Considering the facts, can they be proven wrong? Especially since Atta had even more surprises in store:

> September 19, 2001 (B): Atta's Father
> Claims Son Was Framed
>
> Mohamed Atta's father holds a press conference in Cairo and makes a number of surprising claims. He believes that the Mossad, Israel's spy agency, did the 9/11 attacks, and stole his son's identity. He claims that Atta was a mama's boy prone to airsickness, a dedicated architecture student who rarely mentioned politics, and a victim of an intricate framing. He says that Atta spoke to him on the phone on September 12 about "normal things," one day after he was supposed to be dead.[165]

The September 12 phone call may be mere delusions of a grieving father, but it would have been easy for the FBI to follow up, especially since Egypt is a friendly country: at what time did it happen, from which number, thus from which area (maybe it was

---

165. *The Terror Timeline*, p. 500.

an anonymous number) and how long did the connection last? Such a verification would have found out the father and proven that the call was impossible as his son had perished the day before on Flight AA11, as claimed by the FBI. Yet, as far as we know, this was never done, nor was any intervention requested from their Egyptian counterparts. Should this situation not, at the very least and per criminal investigative protocol, have called for a verification of statements made by the culprits' relatives?

The Terror Timeline continues:

> Atta called his family about once a month, yet never told them he was in the U.S., continuing to say he was studying in Germany. Atta's family never saw him after 1999, and Atta canceled a trip to visit them in late 2000. His father even shows a picture of his son, claiming he looks similar but not the same as the terrorist Atta. (*Newsweek*, 9/24/01; *New York Times*, 9/19/01; *Chicago Tribune*, 9/20/01). He also says that the man pictured in published photos from an airport surveillance camera had a heavier build than his son. (*Cairo Times*, 9/20/01).

The father's statement on the physical difference cannot be considered as evidence, all the more since he supposedly had not seen his son for over a year; his build could have changed. Though, on a passing note, witnesses of the previous years' terrorist attacks in France almost never gave descriptions that fit the men later killed by the police. Still, the reasons behind the FBI's failure to investigate the claims made by Atta's father are indeed puzzling. Were they aware of a fabrication?

This is what Jay Kolar's study suggests in paragraph *2.3 Atta Senior Drops out of Venice Video onto FBI Cutting Room Floor*. According to local independent investigator D. Hopsicker, a pharmacist at the Barclay Pharmacy in Venice, Florida, recognized

Atta's father from the news, and phoned the FBI to let them know he had been there two weeks before 9/11 with his son. Here follows the rest of the story:

> The FBI picked up the pharmacy's security video and later returned it. Contacted by the pharmacist, local independent investigator David Hopsicker (2005a) meticulously examined the videotape and found the splices where the FBI had edited Atta Senior out of the tape for the afternoon of August 28, 2001, effectively erasing the evidence. The FBI has not breathed a word about Atta Senior's short-lived film debut in Florida.

The pharmacist would not be the only witness to have recognized Atta Senior after he went on television:

> [...] according to Hopsicker "a number of credible witnesses called the Sarasota office of the FBI to report they had seen Atta's father in Venice with his son ten days to two weeks before the attack." This is proof that the closed-circuit videotape provided to the FBI as evidence of Atta Senior's presence in Venice two weeks pre-9-11 had its evidence excised. Combine this proof with further local Venice eyewitness accounts that the FBI showed up in Venice, just hours after the attacks, and that the FBI then neglected to inform the 9-11 Commission either about the fact they knew of Atta and company's prolonged presence there before 9-11, or about Mohamed Atta Senior's visit to the US and his stay in Venice, and what we have is corroborating evidence that the FBI not only lied but has also engaged in a massive cover-up.

Further precious information was added by the pharmacist, among which the fact that upon his visit to the pharmacy, Atta's father was accompanied by his son and Marwan al-Shehhi, one of the hijackers of UA175, and

> that Atta Senior had been there to send a fax "to a number in New Jersey." Not only do these disclosures discredit the FBI's official story of Atta's timeline and activities as a story riddled with discrepancies, but they also reveal that the FBI erased and effectively confiscated other information that would show Atta had ties to numerous close non-Arab associates in Florida as well as meetings with visitors from abroad during the final weeks of preparations for the attacks.

It would have been useful to know the number in New Jersey, especially since some of these "close non-Arab associates" may have been linked to drug trafficking. Although this goes beyond the scope of our study, if it turned out to be true, how could the FBI ignore the information? Likewise, if the facts reported in Venice are true, we can only agree with the conclusion of Jay Kolar:

> Atta's father was not the innocently concerned father we saw in interviews after 9-11 denying his son had ever been to the United States or participated in the attacks. In retrospect, Atta Senior is also not the man he pretends to be, and his statement that his son phoned him the day after the attacks, as evidence his son was still alive, cannot be trusted.

However, if the FBI has indeed altered and removed evidence, serious questions once more arise of its true role in 9/11.

FBI's Refusal of DNA Testing

In the same article referred to in the previous section, in question *9. Did DNA Tests Identify Five Hijackers among the Victims at the*

Pentagon?[166], David Griffin reports that DNA analysis done on all victims of Flight AA77 revealed five profiles that did not match with samples given by families. Hence, it was deduced that these profiles were the five hijackers, an assumption that he does not validate:

> We have no way of knowing where these five bodies came from. For the claim that they came from the attack site at the Pentagon, we have only the word of the FBI and the military, which insisted on taking charge of the bodies of everyone killed at the Pentagon and transporting them to the Armed Forces Institute of Pathology.[167]
>
> In any case, the alleged hijackers could have been positively identified only if samples had been obtained from their relatives, and there is no indication that this occurred. Indeed, one can wonder why not. The FBI had lots of information about the men identified as the hijackers. They could easily have located relatives. And these relatives, most of whom reportedly did not believe that their own flesh and blood had been involved in the attacks, would have surely been willing to supply the needed DNA.

In fact, the whole process of identification can be questioned, as noted by Elias Davidsson in his study already cited above:

> According to the official account, the 19 hijackers died in the crashes at the World Trade Center, the Pentagon and at the crash site near Shanksville, Pennsylvania. Yet, there is no positive proof that they did. There is no indication that a

---

166. *Was America Attacked by Muslims on 9/11?*, David Ray Griffin, 9 September 2008, https://www.opednews.com/articles/Was-America-Attacked-by-Mu-by-David-Ray-Griffin-080909-536.html.
167. We will come back with more details on the protocol when it came to the dead (see Chapter *9/11 The FBI Lies*).

proper chain of custody[59] between the crash sites and the final disposition of bodily remains had been established by the FBI, as required in criminal cases. The 9/11 Commission did not refer to any such documentation.

Unidentified officials spoken to by *The Times* (U.K.) in October 2001 *expected* that the bodies of the 9/11 suspects would be identified '[if only] by a process of elimination'[60]. They did not explain why they did not expect a *positive* identification of these bodies.[168]

A *positive* identification means a comparison with DNA samples. It could have been done for the hijackers whose luggage and personal effects had been collected by the FBI, or through items given by cooperating families. Was standard crime-scene procedure respected by the FBI? It certainly looks like it was not the case at the Pentagon. What about the three other flights?

It seems to be the same situation for Ziad Jarrah, the alleged pilot of Flight 93:

Jarrah's family has indicated they would be willing to provide DNA samples to US researchers, [...][but] the FBI has shown no interest thus far.[96]

David Griffin details in note 96 at the end of this sentence that he had sampled the information from the hijacker's Wikipedia page. The passage was deleted in September 2006 and titled *Authority Inconsistencies*. Here is an extract before removal:

The 9/11 Commission concluded that Jarrah was present and behind the controls of the plane when it crashed in an empty field in Shanksville, Pennsylvania. They do not give any

---

168. Note 59: it is the definition of a chain of custody. Note 60: Damian Whitworth, *Hijackers' bodies set Bush grisly ethical question*, *The Times* (U.K.), 6 October 2001.

credence to the idea that Jarrah was not the pilot. Certainly, Jarrah has not been seen since the attacks.

DNA fingerprinting would settle the controversy, as fragmentary remains of all the hijackers have been found. Jarrah's family has indicated they would be willing to provide DNA samples to US researchers, but the FBI has shown no interest thus far.[169]

Reading the complete *Authority Inconsistencies* paragraph is disturbing, as the information does not correspond to the profile of a fanatical jihadist. On the contrary, it even shows that his road to terrorism as explained by John Ashcroft and the FBI is wrong at least in part: he did not study in Hamburg at a school attended by two of the hijackers, nor did he ever live with them. Was it for this reason that the FBI refused to perform DNA testing on the samples that his family was willing to give, to avoid the risk of results contrary to its version of the conspiracy? Unfortunately, it was neither the first time nor the last that the FBI proved reluctant to shed all light on the real events that took place on 9/11.

Could it be that the FBI knew that Ziad Jarrah's case would pose a major problem, as solving it would reveal the use of doubles, dealing a fatal blow to the government narrative?

Identity Fraud and Doppelgangers?

The fact that some were alive after September 11 brings us to the logical conclusion that their identities had been stolen, since, as declared by the FBI, their names were on the manifests. These were not mere likenesses. Photographs and other distinguishing information were also conveyed. However, the travel analysis of several of the hijackers led to the seemingly crazy idea that it was not mere usurpation of identity but the creation of a doubles program, that left many traces:

---

169. https://www.wanttoknow.info/articles/ziad_jarrah

For example, neighbors at the Parkwood Apartments witnessed that Hanjour, al-Hazmi, and al-Mihdhar all remained in San Diego through the month of August up to September 8, 2001. However, these eyewitness accounts are contradicted by other August sightings of them on the opposite coast, obtaining drivers licenses in Falls Church, Virginia, crossing back to Las Vegas, returning across country to Baltimore, and then spending ten days in Newark. How could they be holed up in San Diego while simultaneously crisscrossing the US for the whole month preceding the attacks? Short answer: doubles. The role of doubles sheds significant explanatory light on an entire covert operation of 9/11, which, without the discovery of their existence, would be an impossible riddle.[170]

Jiad Zarrah's case belongs to these "impossible riddles." Of Lebanese origin, several media outlets reported in December 2001 that he had been interrogated during four hours at Dubai airport on January 30, 2001. This was upon his return from Pakistan and Afghanistan where he had spent "the previous two months and five days." After 9/11, investigators confirmed that

> Jarrah had spent at least three weeks in January 2001 at an al-Qaeda training camp in Afghanistan. (CNN, 8/1/2002).[171]

What luck, a hijacker trained under bin Laden! This prompt information came a few weeks after *9/11 The Big Lie* and *Pentagate* were published, which challenged the government version of the conspiracy, with an article in the *New York Times* on June 22, 2002. However, this "official" schedule of Ziad Jarrah contradicted other statements as the one of the flight school where he trained, the Florida Flight Training Center, which confirmed that he was there

---

170. *What We Know About the Alleged 9/11 Hijackers*, Jay Kolar, p. 22.
171. *The Terror Timeline*, p. 192.

until January 15, 2001. Obviously, he could not have simultaneously been in Florida and an Al-Qaeda camp in Afghanistan. Furthermore, his family declared that he had arrived in Lebanon on January 26 to be with his father who had just undergone open-heart surgery, and that he visited him in the hospital every day until after January 30. This eliminates the possibility of the Dubai interrogation.

It would have been easy for the FBI to check if Ziad Jarrah was in Florida until January 15 before leaving for Lebanon. It has not been done, despite his memory being weighed down by heavy accusations. It also means that one culprit is yet to be identified.

According to the information that CNN received from the Emirates and European intelligence sources:

> The questioning of Jarrah fits a pattern of a CIA operation begun in 1999 to track suspected al-Qaeda operatives who were traveling through the United Arab Emirates. These sources told CNN that UAE officials were often told in advance by US officials which persons were coming through the country and whom they wanted questioned. One source provided CNN a drawing of the Dubai airport and described how people wanted for questioning were intercepted, most often at a transit desk. US officials declined to comment on whether the CIA operated this way at the Dubai airport. (MacVicar& Faraj, 2002).[172]

During his interrogation, the Ziad Jarrah double said that he would return to Florida, but did not board his KLM flight to Europe the day after. This story proves that the CIA lied when they declared that they had not known of Ziad Jarrah before 9/11 and had no reason to watch him, as was confirmed by an Emirati executive:

---

172. *What We Now Know about the Alleged 9-11 Hijackers*, Jay Kolar, p. 23.

"The Americans told us that he was a supporter of terrorist organizations, that he had connections with terrorist organizations," the source said. "His name was given to us as someone to check. The US said he should be questioned. He was questioned at the request of the US."[173]

Another point is worth being outlined: all published photos of Ziad Jarrah are consistent, except the one on his passport, which miraculously survived to the crash of Flight 93 and had burnt just enough (we will come back to this "unbelievable" discovery in chapter *9/9 The FBI Forged False Evidence?*).

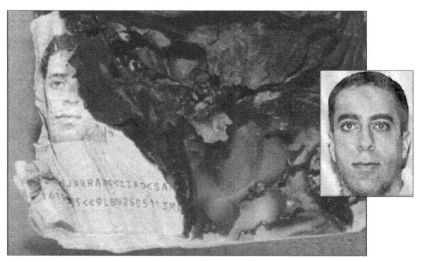

Left: "A partly-burned copy of Ziad Jarrah's U.S. visa recovered from the Flight 93 crash site in Somerset County, Pennsylvania."
By chance, the unscathed part of the passport was the right one.
Right: the picture of Ziad Jarrah's driving license, issued on May 2, 2001, communicated by the Florida Department of Highway Safety and Motor Vehicles.
In comparing it with the one on the passport found by the FBI, one wonders if it is the same person or a forgery "made in FBI"?

---

173. *What We Now Know about the Alleged 9-11 Hijackers*, Jay Kolar, p. 24.

More Doppelgangers?

In his analysis of the footage referred to earlier, allegedly taken at the Dulles Airport by a surveillance camera, David Griffin studies the specific case of Hani Hanjour:

> Another problem with this so-called Dulles video is that, although one of the men on it was identified by the 9/11 Commission as Hani Hanjour,[75] he "does not remotely resemble Hanjour." Whereas Hanjour was thin and had a receding hairline (as shown by a photo taken six days before 9/11), the man in the video had a somewhat muscular build and a full head of hair, with no receding hairline.[76]174

Jay Kolar draws the following conclusion:

> Thus the discrepancy is striking: it is not Hanjour at all in the photo from the Dulles video.[175]

Hani Hanjour is not the only questionable figure on the Dulles video:

> The presence of Salem al-Hazmi allegedly preparing to board Flight 77 introduces a *second* problem: both he and al-Mihdhar could not have boarded that flight since they were reported alive after 9-11, and yet they, of all five "hijackers," are perhaps the most clearly identifiable in the Dulles video images which bear close resemblance to their FBI photographs.[176]

---

174. *7. Were al-Qaeda Operatives Captured on Airport Security Videos?*, in *Was America Attacked by Muslims on 9/11?*, David Griffin. Notes 75 et 76 : 75. 9/11CR 452n11.

76. Jay Kolar, *What We Now Know about the Alleged 9-11 Hijackers*, in Paul Zarembka, Emerald Group Publishing, *The Hidden History of 9-11* (New York: Seven Stories, 2008), 3-44, at 8 (emphasis Kolar's).

175. *What We Now Know about the Alleged 9-11 Hijackers*, Jay Kolar, p. 9.

176. *What We Now Know about the Alleged 9-11 Hijackers*, Jay Kolar, p. 7.

Indeed, Salem al-Hazmilater later declared that he never went to the United States and that he has been at work at the time, in the Saudi petrochemical complex of Yanbou. Besides, he was alive. Thus, it cannot be him in the video, despite the uncanny resemblance. Finally, Jay Kolar raises five inconsistencies in this Dulles video, leading to the following conclusion:

> The government's case that the "hijackers" were agents of bin Laden's al-Qaeda had as its best evidence the Dulles video purportedly showing them preparing to board the plane which crashed into the Pentagon. All five of our problems with the evidence combine to undermine the Dulles video's authenticity and corroborate its forgery. It is the flimsiest evidence upon which the entire weight of the official story collapses. No airport security video has appeared for the other flights. Therefore, no evidence exists that any of the "hijackers" ever boarded planes that crashed on 9/11.[177]

It is not, however, "the flimsiest evidence upon which the entire weight of the official story collapses," as will be shown throughout the study. Even the Hani Hanjour case is apparently so weak that the FBI pulled all the tricks to convince that the Saudi was the pilot of Flight 77. Mark H. Gaffney states in his article *How the FBI and 9/11 Commission Suppressed Key Evidence about Hani Hanjour, alleged hijack pilot of AAL 77*:

> The FBI file also conspicuously fails to mention the Jet Tech instructor's [negative] written evaluation of Hani Hanjour's flying skills. The omission easily qualifies as suppression of evidence because we know the FBI had the document in its possession. It was made public at the trial of Zacharias Moussaoui when the document was submitted as evidence.

---

177. *What We Now Know about the Alleged 9-11 Hijackers*, Jay Kolar, p. 10.

This means, of course that the 9/11 Commission also surely had it and similarly suppressed it.[178]

Mark H. Gaffney adds that close inspection of the FBI file also shows "that someone padded the record to put the best face on Hanjour's flight training." He investigated further at Freeway airport and interviewed two flight instructors after the FBI. Both confirmed Hanjour's lack of piloting prowess:

> The file also conspicuously fails to mention that Hanjour flunked his test flight evaluation! Whether through incompetence or deception, the FBI failed on every point to state the facts correctly.

This flunked test happened shortly before September 11, and still the government version of the conspiracy will have us believe that Hanjour was the pilot of Flight 77? Here is what two professional pilots, among many others, make of it:

> Philip Marshall, who is licensed to fly Boeing 727s, 737s, 747s, as well as 757s and 767s, recently authored a book, False Flag 911, in which he states categorically that the alleged 9/11 hijacker pilots, including Hani Hanjour, could never have flown 767s and 757s into buildings at high speed without advanced training and practice flights in that same aircraft over a period of months. As Marshall put it: "Hitting a 90-foot target [i.e., the Pentagon] with a 757 at 500 mph is extremely difficult— absolutely impossible for first-time fliers of a heavy airliner.[179]

---

178. *How the FBI and 9/11 Commission Suppressed Key Evidence about Hani Hanjour, alleged hijack pilot of AAL 77, alleged hijack pilot of AAL 77*, Mark H. Gaffney, July 7, 2009, http://911truth.org/hani-hanjour-evidence-suppressed-fbi-commission/.

179. *How the FBI and 9/11 Commission Suppressed Key Evidence about Hani Hanjour, alleged hijack pilot of AAL 77, alleged hijack pilot of AAL 77*, Mark H. Gaffney.

A 35-year veteran Pan Am and United jetliner pilot, Russ Wittenberg claimed that the Boeing airliners could not have performed the high-speed maneuvers the government said they did, *no matter who flew them* (Szymanski, 2005). Wittenberg convincingly argued it was not possible for Flight 77 to have "descended 7,000 feet in two minutes, all the while performing a steep 270 degree banked turn before crashing into the Pentagon's first floor wall without touching the lawn" (Szymanski, 2005). According to Wittenberg, no amount of experience flying commercial jetliners could have helped to accomplish such a high-speed maneuver without stalling the Boeing and sending it into a nosedive.[180]

The final chapter will further build on this point. In any case, it is clear that despite the presentation made by the FBI, and even if he obtained a flight certificate on September 10[181], Hani Hanjour had no 757 practice and would have been utterly incapable of maneuvering Flight 77 as described in the government version.

Mark H. Gaffney then raises another interesting point:

The record indicates that on September 5, 2001, just six days before 9/11, Hanjour showed up at the First Union National Bank in Laurel, Maryland where he made four failed bank transactions. The file cites bank records showing that Hanjour was unable to make balance inquiries and withdraw funds from his account because he failed to enter the correct pin number, which he evidently had forgotten! Two days later, Hanjour returned to the bank, this time accompanied by an unidentified male, and made another unsuccessful attempt to withdraw $4,900.

---

180. *What We Now Know about the Alleged 9-11 Hijackers*, Jay Kolar, p. 20.
181. *American Airlines Flight 77*, https://en.wikipedia.org/wiki/American_Airlines_Flight_77.

It is astonishing the FBI file was ever touted as authenticating Hanjour's flight credentials. The document falls short on that score and actually raises new questions.

Namely, did Hani Hanjour really forget his pin number or was it his double? If the existence of doubles is confirmed, at least for some of the hijackers identified by the FBI, multiple questions would be raised. For example, who piloted Flight 77? What happened to the real Ziad Jarrah, Hani Hanjour...? Etc.

Crackdowns on Muslims

In disregard of their fundamental rights, hundreds of Muslims were arrested in the aftermath of 9/11 and held "incommunicado" (without the means or the right to communicate). At least 762 detainees would be swept up nationwide, including 491 in the New York area; locked up between three and eight months on average, abused, with solitary confinement 23 hours a day, regular strip searches with humiliating sexual comments and insults to their religion, physical violence, and the list goes on.[182]

Legal authorities justified these measures by claiming that they would help prevent and deter further attacks. However, after reading the previous pages, it becomes hard to believe the government narrative of 9/11 with Islamic terrorists from Al-Qaeda.

In this anti-Muslim context, a testimony about the Dulles video particularly drew our attention:

> Airport security manager Ed Nelson describes the FBI confiscating this video some time after 10:00 A.M. on 9/11 saying: "They pulled the tape right away... They knew who the hijackers were out of hundreds of people going through

---

182. *Lawsuit brought by Muslims rounded up after 9/11 gets go-ahead from court*, *The Guardian*, from Associated Press New York, June 21, 2015.

the checkpoints… **It boggles my mind that they had already had the hijackers identified**… Both metal detectors were open at that time, and lots of traffic was moving through. So picking people out is hard… I wanted to know how they had that kind of information."[35][183]

The answers of these FBI agents would be significant, but there is little chance of ever getting them. In the meantime, Ed Nelson's statement has us posit: what if they did not rush to the airport after having identified the hijackers but to look for Muslim faces to make up the "kamikaze team"? It would mean that they have arrested innocent people afterwards, with fatal consequences. This strange hypothesis would explain some inconsistencies and anomalies, but also why the FBI forbade the publication of initial passenger lists and classified the Dulles video of which the original version was never released—something that the FBI has made a habit of, as will be shown hereafter.

Here is how Elias Davidsson concludes his study that was quoted previously:

As shown above, the US authorities have failed to prove that the 19 individuals accused of the mass murder of 9/11 had boarded the aircraft, which they allegedly used to commit the crime. No authenticated, original, passenger lists, bearing their names, have been released; no one is known to have seen them board the aircraft; no video recordings documented their boarding; no boarding pass stub is known to exist; and there is no proof that the alleged hijackers actually died at the known crash sites, because their bodily remains were not

183. In bold in the text. Source: http://arabesque911.blogspot. com/2008/08/911-misinformation-flight-passenger.html, August 28, 2008.
Note 35: Susan B. Trento and Joseph J. Trento, *Unsafe at any Altitude: Failed Terrorism Investigations, Scapegoating 9/11, and the Shocking Truth about Aviation Security Today*, Steerforth Publishing, October 3, 2006, p. 37.

positively identified and the chain-of-custody of these remains was broken. [...]

Some people may wonder why the U.S. government has not simply faked all necessary evidence, such as "authentic passenger lists," fake testimonies and fake boarding passes, in order to prove its allegations. One can only conjecture why this has not been done. Perhaps the U.S. government found that this would require the criminal participation of too many individuals, something that would be riskier than simply avoid mentioning these issues in the first place. Until now the U.S. government could rely on mass media to ask no questions about the lack of evidence.[184]

So could the FBI. Maybe this will change. Only this time it will not be the mainstream media asking the real questions, which they have not done for eighteen years, but the American people.

Expect a somewhat different answer.

---

184. *There is no evidence that Muslims hijacked planes on 9/11*, Elias Davidsson, January 10, 2008, pp. 10-11.

The hole by which entered and disappeared the "aircraft."

Even the lawn is intact.

The FBI Buried

Five Pictures and Nothing Else

One of the mysteries surrounding 9/11 is the lack of visual material showing what happened in Washington, as if, on that specific day, no cameras were working. Even after the attack on the Pentagon we saw close to nothing on TV, whereas the World Trade Center was broadcast over and over.

Controversy grew with Thierry Meyssan's website showing the impossibility that a Boeing crashed into the Pentagon's facade. Fittingly, in March 2002, CNN announced an imminent release of images taken by a nearby parking lot security camera, saying it would prove beyond any doubt that it was flight AA77. Then began the waiting process, because if the images undeniably conveyed the presence of an airliner, the government version would have become almost unquestionable, albeit despite many remaining inconsistencies.

On March 7, 2002, five images were released. Why only five? Why not the entire clip? Whatever the reason, the pictures in no way proved the presence of a Boeing 757. In fact, one could even conclude the opposite: "No plane crashed into the Pentagon."[185] How could CNN, the broadcaster of these five pictures, assert that it is undoubtedly Flight 77? Maybe CNN switched from "Cable News Network" to "Cover-up News Network"—over the years it seems this has not improved, with the channel sometimes nicknamed "FNN" for "Fraud News Network" or "Fake News Network."

Nevertheless, should we accept that, apart from the security camera, nobody filmed what happened? In Washington DC, a city

---

185. Catchphrase of the French version of *9/11 The Big Lie.*

with one of the densest networks of close circuit surveillance in the world? Of course not, because the FBI was watching.

The Pentagon Gas Station Tapes

On December 11, 2001, the *Richmond Times* reported that journalist Bill McKelway interviewed José Velasquez, attendant at the gas station Nexcomm/Citgo, on what happened just after the Pentagon attack:

> An employee at a gas station across the street from the Pentagon that services only military personnel says the gas station's security camera should have recorded the moment of impact. However, he says, "I've never seen what the pictures looked like. The FBI was here within minutes and took the film."[186]

In this specific case, the FBI operated surprisingly fast, as if it were the most urgent step. Then again, it is normal that investigators took the tapes to shed light on the crime they were dealing with.

The Commission, however, did not mention these tapes, as if they did not exist. David Griffin reckons that it should have auditioned gas station attendant José Velasquez, journalist Bill McKelway, and the agents who seized the tapes to know who had given the order and when. Why did they arrive at the gas station "within minutes" to seize the tapes? The Commission also should have asked the FBI to hand back the tapes, but nothing is mentioned in the *Report*.

Takeover at the Sheraton

The gas station was not alone in receiving a hasty visit from FBI agents immediately after the Pentagon attack. *The Gertz Files* published the following information on September 21, 2001:

---

186. *The 9/11 Commission Report – Omissions and Distortions*, David Griffin, p. 38.

Now word has reached us that federal investigators may have video footage of the deadly terrorist attack on the Pentagon.

A security camera atop a hotel close to the Pentagon may have captured dramatic footage of the hijacked Boeing 757 airliner as it slammed into the western wall of the Pentagon. Hotel employees sat watching the film in shock and horror several times before the FBI confiscated the video as part of its investigation.

It may be the only available video of the attack.[187]

Indeed, *The Gertz Files* added:

The Pentagon has told broadcast news reporters that its security cameras did not capture the crash.

The attack occurred close to the Pentagon's heliport, an area that normally would be under 24-hour security surveillance, including video monitoring.

The author is surprised that no Pentagon cameras filmed the attack, but since the military made the statement, we just had to take their word for it. So, if we want to see what happened, the only remaining option is the confiscated footage from the hotel. Soon after, the Sheraton National Hotel was revealed as the owner of the tapes. If the claim that "hotel employees sat watching the film in shock and horror several times" is true, there is no doubt that the scene had been recorded.

Consequently, this is the video that CNN should have been given in the first place. Of course, as it should not be anything other than AA77 crashing into the Pentagon, it would have confirmed the government version of 9/11 once for all. Yet, all viewers were granted were five measly images taken from the Pentagon parking

187. Inside the Ring, *The Gertz Files*, 09/21/2001, http://web.archive.org/web/20021219062257/http://www.gertzfile.com/gertzfile/ring092101.html.

lot. Why? Did the Sheraton tape show a different story? What has become of it after all these years? The 9/11 Commission *Report* made no mention of the tape, when its contents could be crucial in understanding what really happened.

It should be added that other footage could also have been telling. As an example, the Virginia Department of Transportation has a view that may have offered important footage. Like the Sheraton National tapes, it seems it has never been publicly broadcast.

In short, by the end of March 2002, six months after the events, the only available images from Washington were the five pictures from the Pentagon parking lot.

Four years later, there has been little change, as stated by the 9-11 Research website on its *Pentagon Attack Footage* page:

> It is striking that there is neither video footage nor any photographic evidence in the public domain showing a jetliner approaching or crashing into the Pentagon. As of May 2006, the only video footage of the crash that has been released are clips from two Pentagon security cameras north of the crash site, one the source of 5 frames leaked in 2002.
>
> With the release of the two video clips, the Pentagon claims to have supplied all of the footage it has of the attack. Although the number and positions of security cameras monitoring the Pentagon is not public knowledge, it seems unlikely that only two security cameras captured the attack. Isn't it reasonable to assume that there were dozens, if not hundreds, of security cameras ringing the huge building that is the heart of the United States military establishment?[188]

---

188. 9-11 Research, *Pentagon Attack Footage*, http://911research.wtc7.net/pentagon/evidence/footage.html.

Double Ration for Hotels

The United States passed an important democratic law, the Freedom of Information Act (FOIA)[189], which allows information to be requested from the government and more than 100 agencies. As the FBI confiscated the tapes and kept them secret, a FOIA request was the only solution to get a copy, albeit with no guarantee of a result.

In February 2002, CNN Senior Pentagon Correspondent Jamie McIntyre learnt from the manager of the Doubletree Hotel in Arlington that he too had his tape confiscated by the FBI. CNN management decided to deliver a FOIA request to get a copy. It was, however, denied because at the time the tape was considered evidence in the Zacarias Moussaoui investigation.

The 9-11 Research website provides a complete timeline for two other FOIA requests—there may have been more—on its *Pentagon Attack Footage* page:

> October 14, 2004: Scott A. Hodes, on behalf of his client Scott Bingham, sends a request to David Hardy of the FBI requesting any videos "that may have captured the impact of Flight 77 into the Pentagon on September 11, 2001." The request letter mentions videotapes from the Citgo Gas Station and the Sheraton National Hotel.
> November 3, 2004: The FBI replies to Bingham's request stating that their search "revealed no record responsive to your FOIA request".

Such an answer looks like a denial of the tapes' existence and reveals evidence of obstruction and lies by the FBI, an institution entrusted with law enforcement.

---

189. "The Freedom of Information Act (FOIA), 5 U.S.C. § 552, is a federal freedom of information law that requires the full or partial disclosure of previously unreleased information and documents controlled by the United States government upon request." https://en.wikipedia.org/wiki/Freedom_of_Information_Act_(United_States)

November 17, 2004: Hodes files an appeal of Bingham's FOIA request with the U.S Department of Justice (DOJ), citing evidence that the videotapes mentioned in the original request exist.

December 15, 2004: Christopher J. Farrell of Judicial Watch, Inc. writes to James Hogan in the Office of Freedom of Information/Security Review of the DOD requesting that the U.S. Department of Homeland Security (DHS), DOD, and FBI produce any and all agency records concerning, relating to, or reflecting the following subjects:

(1) Video camera recordings obtained by federal official(s) and/or law enforcement from a Nexcomm/Citgo gas station in the vicinity of the Pentagon on or about September 11, 2001.

(2) Pentagon security video camera recording(s) showing Flight 77 strike and/or hit and/or crash into the Pentagon on September 11, 2001.

(3) Closed Circuit Television (CCTV) video camera recording(s) obtained by any federal official(s) and/or law enforcement from the Virginia Department of Transportation ("VDOT") and/or the VDOT "Smart Traffic Center" on or about September 11, 2001.[190]

Regarding the footage, after a rough start to 2005 spent wrestling with the Department of Justice (DoJ) and the Department of Defense (DoD), the situation improved. On September 7, 2005, Special Agent Jacqueline Maguire, assigned to the Counterterrorism Division of the FBI's Washington Field Office, signed a declaration. She had been asked to determine whether the FBI possessed any videotapes that may have captured the impact of Flight 77 into the Pentagon:

---

190. 9-11 Research, *Pentagon Attack Footage*, http://911research.wtc7.net/pentagon/evidence/footage.html.

[...] 9. On April 4, 2005, [...] In particular, I was asked to determine whether the FBI possessed any videotapes from a Citgo Gas Station, or any gas station, or a Sheraton Hotel, or any hotel, that showed Flight 77 on September 11, 2001.

10. On April 6, 2005, I responded [...] that although the FBI possessed other videotapes that depicted the Pentagon on September 11, 2001, those videotapes depicted only post-impact scenes and, therefore, did not show the impact of Flight 77 into the Pentagon.

11. In response to follow-up questions from RMD [Records Management Division] personnel, I subsequently searched a series of FBI evidence databases, including the FBI's Electronic Case File System and the FBI's Investigative Case Management System, and determined that the FBI possessed eighty-five (85) videotapes that might be potentially responsive to plaintiff's FOIA request. This determination was based on videotapes that had been submitted into FBI evidence, sent directly to the FBI laboratory in Quantico, Virginia, and/or obtained by the FBI's Washington Field Office.

12. I next determined, through an examination of the chain of custody and other written supporting documentation associated with each videotape, that fifty-six (56) of these videotapes did not show either the Pentagon building, the Pentagon crash site, or the impact of Flight 77 into the Pentagon on September 11, 2001.

13. I personally viewed the remaining twenty-nine (29) videotapes. I determined that sixteen (16) of these videotapes did not show the Pentagon crash site and did not show the impact of Flight 77 into the Pentagon on September 11, 2001.

14. Out of the remaining thirteen (13} videotapes, which did show the Pentagon crash site, twelve (12) videotapes only showed the Pentagon after the impact of Flight 77. I determined that only one videotape showed the impact of Flight 77 into

the Pentagon on September 11, 2001. That videotape is the CD-ROM described in paragraph 23 of the Hardy Declaration, dated August 1, 2005.

15. Among the eighty-five (85) videotapes described in paragraph 11, above, I located one videotape taken from closed circuit television at the Citgo Gas Station in Arlington, Virginia. Because of its generally poor quality, this tape was taken to the FBI's Forensic Audio-Video Image Analysis Unit ("FAVIAU") by another member of the PENTTBOM Investigative Team. FAVIAU was requested to determine whether the videotape showed the impact of Flight 77 into the Pentagon on September 11, 2001 and, if such evidence existed on the videotape, to develop still photographic images of it. Personnel from FAVIAU assisted personnel from the PENTTBOM Investigative Team to determine that the videotape did not show the impact of Flight 77 into the Pentagon on September 11, 2001.

16. I also conducted a search of the FBI's Electronic Case File system, Investigative Case Management system, and other evidence databases for any videotapes in the possession of the FBI from the Sheraton National Hotel in Arlington, Virginia. I did not locate any such videotape.

I did locate one videotape taken from a closed-circuit television at a Doubletree Hotel in Arlington, Virginia. I determined, however, that the videotape did not show the impact of Flight 77 into the Pentagon on September 11, 2001.[191]

Eighty-five videos in the FBI's possession, but none show the impact of Flight 77 (except the parking lot camera). The Sheraton National Hotel footage that "hotel employees sat watching in shock and horror several times" does not feature in the FBI database. It

---

191. http://www.judicialwatch.org/wp-content/uploads/2013/07/A_2006_double-treeaffadavit.pdf.

disappeared, purposely or through neglect. In both cases it should cause problems for the FBI.

As for the Virginia Department of Transportation clip, requested by Judicial Watch through the FOIA, Jacqueline Maguire's declaration did not mention it either. This too is highly disappointing, since the building is located along the flight's trajectory and therefore should have provided a solid angle.

What Was Supposed to Happen Happened

After a lawsuit concluded that the DoD had "no legal basis" in its refusal to release the footage, four tapes were made available on the Judicial Watch website:

1. Pentagon security cameras footage #1;
2. Pentagon security cameras footage #2;
3. Footage from the Citgo cameras;
4. Footage from the Doubletree cameras.

The first two videos have been discussed and the third offers no useful information. CNN stated the following on the fourth clip:

> There was speculation that this video might show the American Airlines 757 jetliner before it crashed, but a close examination by CNN only revealed the subsequent explosion and no image of the jet.[192]

CNN is right. We cannot discern the plane as the crash occurred on the opposite side of the Pentagon hidden from the camera. Yet, it was in the flight path. However, the most important in this video does not seem to be what we see but what we cannot see. Indeed, since the video starts a fraction of a second before impact,

---

192. http://edition.cnn.com/2006/WORLD/europe/12/02/saturday/index.html.

a few additional seconds would normally allow us to see the plane zoning in on the Pentagon since it did not nosedive. Did the original recording start a second before impact, or was it edited by the FBI?

There is a seemingly boundless sea of bad luck surrounding the Washington tapes. The promising Hotel Sheraton footage was somehow misplaced by the FBI; they avoided mentioning the Virginia Department of Transportation recording; the two parking lot cameras do not show the precise moment of impact; the last tape unfortunately starts only a second before impact and therefore contains no relevant information. And to top it all off is the fact that so little "relevant" footage was captured in the first place despite Washington supposedly being the world capital.

Minutes After Disaster

Pictures were taken a few minutes after the attack, before the facade collapsed (see p. 135). This study does not focus on the controversy surrounding the impact zone, but we will leave the reader with the following words from François Grangier, air crash investigation expert, flight commander, instructor and flight examiner:

> What is certain when one looks at the photo of this façade that remains intact is that it is obvious the plane did not go through there. We can imagine that a plane of such a size cannot pass through a window and leave the frame still standing. But it is obvious that if there was a plane, it must have hit somewhere else.[193]

It is precisely this observation that convinced me to propose Thierry Meyssan to write *9/11 The Big Lie* then *Pentagate*. A Boeing 757 cannot disappear through a six-meter-wide hole on the ground floor without any other damage to the building or even the lawn, which remained intact. This does not seem to be the FBI's opinion, but we will come back on Flight 77 in the final chapter.

---

193. + Clair, Canal + (televised news program), March 23, 2002, in *Pentagate*, p. 36.

The Anthrax Case

From September 18, 2001, i.e. seven days after the attacks, envelopes containing deadly anthrax spores were sent by mail. The first recipients were mainstream media, before Democrat Senators Patrick Leahy and Tom Daschle were targeted in October. Five people were killed and some twenty more infected. The spores used in the last two letters were so sophisticated that Hart Senate Office Building had to be closed during several months for decontamination. Because of the text and context, al-Qaeda was immediately suspected, followed by Iraq, then both, as only a State could produce such a complex bioweapon.

Although every effort was made to advocate the "foreign enemy" hypothesis, independent scientists demonstrated soon after that the strains incontrovertibly came from American military laboratories or Pentagon subcontractors. Therefore, the Muslim lead should be excluded. However, civilian casualties were not the only objective, as stated by Prof. Graeme McQueen:

> What were the effects of the anthrax attacks and who was the perpetrator?
> The main effect was to keep up the momentum established by the 9/11 attacks. The external aspect of the reaction to 9/11 was directed toward those thought responsible: this reaction supported the invasion and occupation of Afghanistan. The first bombs were dropped on Afghanistan on October 7, 2001, two days after the first death in the U.S. from anthrax. The anthrax attacks kept al-Qaeda and Afghanistan in the crosshairs.[194]

Prof. Graeme McQueen added that the preparations for Iraq invasion in 2003 had begun during this period. Indeed, Senator John

---

194. *9/11 Truth: War on Terror or "War on Democracy"? The Physical Intimidation of Legislatures, Prof. Graeme McQueen*, Global Research, September 08, 2018.

McCain announced on television on October 18, 2001, that after Afghanistan, "the second phase is Iraq."[195] But it was domestically where the anthrax affair had been most successful:

> Attorney General John Ashcroft had introduced what would later be called the Patriot Act shortly after 9/11 and had made it clear to Congress that he wanted it passed immediately. But there was resistance. Both the population at large and Congress began to recover from the 9/11 attacks, and as they did so their willingness to sacrifice civil rights began to diminish. The anthrax attacks saved the day for Ashcroft by ensuring that both population and Congress remained sufficiently intimidated to accept the Patriot act. The act was passed on October 26, 2001. The connection between its passage and the anthrax attacks is very clear.
>
> There were two powerful Democratic senators whose actions were slowing down passage of the Patriot Act. One was Tom Daschle, whom I have mentioned previously. The second was Patrick Leahy, Chair of the Senate Judiciary Committee. Anthrax letters were sent out to Daschle and Leahy immediately after they resisted a deadline for passage of the bill proposed by Vice-President Dick Cheney.
>
> How odd that al-Qaeda and Iraq would have had a special hatred of Democratic senators who slowed down the Patriot Act!
>
> But, of course, the anthrax letters were not sent by al-Qaeda and Iraq. According to what we have since learned, no Muslim had anything whatsoever to do with the attacks.
>
> [...] the lies pushed in October-November of 2001 to frame Afghanistan and Iraq for the anthrax attacks (Iraq as sponsor, al-Qaeda as client) belonged to the same repository of lies

195. *October 18, 2001:Senator McCain Says Second Phase of War on Terrorism is Iraq, Suggests Iraq May Be Responsible for Anthrax Attacks*, HistoryCommons.org.

that was used over a period of years to justify the 2003 attack on Iraq. The two main deceptions were (a) that Iraq had "weapons of mass destruction" and (b) that Iraq was a sponsor of al-Qaeda.

The investigation was entrusted to the FBI and would drag on for seven years. It surfaced as early as October 2001 that the source of the spores was undoubtedly American and close to the military. This left at most a dozen laboratories—among them the USAMRIID, the US Army's main facility for research on biological warfare at Fort Detrick, Maryland—and between one and two hundred scientists. Despite the limited number of suspects, FBI auditions still had not been completed six months later, which stirred up confusion, as if it did not want the case to be solved. Could it be that the culprits were American and linked to the military? Despite not having a fraction of proof and much like the announcements made in the wake of 9/11:

> The FBI then quickly claimed that an individual was responsible for the attacks and began noisily looking for this "lone wolf."[196]

As such, several successive suspects were identified with some of them thrown in the media and public lion's cage. For example, the FBI investigated three Pakistani-born individuals working in Chester, Pennsylvania. Naturally, their deadly anthrax producing skills were lacking, but still the FBI had no scruples in sticking them on the front page and forever obliterating their reputations. Two of them saw their applications for US citizenship refused and had to leave the US when their visas ran out. As for the third man, already a US citizen, he was put on a no-fly watch list for six years, bringing with it endless administrative and security hassles.

---

196. *The 2001 Anthrax Deception: The Case For a Domestic Conspiracy, Graeme MacQueen,* Clarity Press, 2014.

Three scientists were also victims of FBI bullying tactics, with one of them, Steven Hatfield, eventually receiving nearly $6 million in compensation from the government after the FBI had ruined his career and reputation. Yet, he was never arrested or even indicted, because there was not the slightest hint of proof or a testimonial against him. The two other scientists, Perry Mikesell[197] and Bruce Edwards Ivins, chose to end their own lives by committing suicide.

After the latter's death on July 29, 2008, the FBI classed the anthrax case as solved. However, many of his colleagues claimed that he lacked the knowledge to produce such a powder and did not picture him as a terrorist. Furthermore, what could have been his motives in committing such a crime? Why would he have sent deadly letters to two senators opposing the Patriot Act? What is striking once again are the methods and tactics of the FBI in pushing around the defenseless. For example, we learn that:

> FBI agents are pressuring Ivins in public places and also pressuring his children. At some point in March, when Ivins is at a shopping mall with his wife and son, FBI agents confronted him, saying, "You killed a bunch of people." Then they turn to his wife and say, "Do you know he killed people?" That same week, Ivins angrily tells a former colleague that he suspects his therapist is cooperating with the FBI. [*Washington Post, 8/6/2008*] Such public pressuring of Ivins's family members had begun by late autumn 2007.[198]

There is little doubt that Ivins was a troubled man. Though whether he became troubled enough to kill himself before or

---

197. "According to family members, he begins drinking heavily after the FBI starts suspecting him, consuming up to a fifth of hard liquor a day. One relative will later say, 'It was a shock that all of a sudden he's a raging alcoholic.' He dies in late October 2002. The relative will say, 'He drank himself to death.'" Source: *Late October 2002: Anthrax Attacks Suspect Drinks Himself to Death,* HistoryCommons.org.
198. *March 2008: FBI Agents Pressure Anthrax Attacks Suspect Ivins and His Family*, HistoryCommons.org.

after the relentless hounding of investigators (who showed photos of anthrax victims to his daughter and declared "your father did this" and fruitlessly offered $2.5m to his son as enticement to turn on his own father) is yet another open question.[199]

He had just been released from a psychiatric hospital in which he stayed from July 10 to July 23.[200] Brad Friedman, in his *The Guardian* article quoted in the previous paragraph, noted that the FBI persisted even after Ivins's death:

> The case against Dr Bruce Ivins—the widely-respected bio-terror researcher at the US army's medical research institute of infectious disease [USAMRIID] in Fort Detrick, Maryland—was revealed by the FBI in a press conference, following his reported suicide the previous week, several ensuing days of bad reporting, laughable evidence-free leaks from anonymous government officials to media outlets happy to repeat them, growing scepticism from experts in the field of bio-terror research, colleagues of Ivins and anybody who bothered to pay close attention beyond the misleading headlines.
>
> The trouble began to reveal itself on the Friday, the same day Ivins' death was first reported, when experts in the field of bio-terror research noted one simple point: Ivins, the FBI's latest supposed "Anthrax Killer" (they had just settled a lawsuit with their last one, Steven Hatfill, in June, to the tune of $[5,82]m dollars) had "no access to dry, powdered anthrax" at the Fort Detrick facility.

199.'*Anthrax killer' remains a mystery*, Brad Friedman, *The Guardian*, 11 Aug 2008.
200. *July 23, 2008: Anthrax Attacks Suspect Ivins Released from Mental Hospital; FBI Does Not Arrest Him*, HistoryCommons.org.

Furthermore, colleagues of his claimed, had he tried to create any from the liquid version kept at the facility, he'd not have been able to do so without being noticed. Even after the FBI finally released a limited subset of one-sided information on Wednesday, the scepticism from experts and peers has persisted.

In order to dispel doubts and prove its theory, the FBI contracted the National Science Academy for a study. But they found that FBI science could not establish a conclusive link between Ivins and the source of the 2001 attacks' anthrax spores.[201]

Nevertheless, the case was already closed and Robert Mueller, Director of the FBI, declared a few days after the suicide of Bruce Edwards Ivins:

> "I do not apologize for any aspect of the investigation." It is erroneous "to say there were mistakes."[202]

If the objective had been to find "a lone wolf" and, in doing so, hide the true culprits, no mistakes were indeed made. It had even been a massive success: the culprit chosen by the FBI would never speak again. Mission accomplished.

---

201. *February 15, 2011: FBI-Funded Anthrax Science Review Does Not Find Conclusive Link to Ivins*, HistoryCommons.org.
202. *August 8, 2008: FBI Director Mueller Says No Mistakes Were Made in Anthrax Attacks Investigation*, HistoryCommons.org.

Chapter 9/8

The FBI Let Disappear

The Rubble of the World Trade Center

This part main will not address the crucial inconsistencies and anomalies regarding events in New York City, such as the near-instant crumbling of the towers in ten seconds; the explosions heard by the firemen just before, corroborated by witnesses like WTC janitor William Rodriguez, who confirmed it to me in May 2005 and further validated by seismic monitoring; who warned Mayor Rudolph Giuliani and his team that the towers were about to collapse, whereas it is unpredictable and rescuers still kept rushing up the stairs; why did Larry Silverstein and the firemen "pull" WTC 7 when low-intensity fires on the 7th and 12th floors posed no structural threat; etc.

Although fundamental, these points did not interest the Commission or the FBI. Nonetheless, they render the government version impossible. There would at least have been some form of explosives, and not only in Tower 7, which would explain the eyewitness accounts mentioned above.

With this book nearing its end, good news has been received from the United States. The US Attorney for the Southern District of New York informed the 9/11 Lawyers Committee that he has accepted to submit their request to a grand jury for yet-to-be prosecuted crimes related to the use of pre-planted explosives and/or incendiaries to destroy WTC1, WTC2 and WTC7. At long last, the first step towards an independent investigation into the events of September 11, 2001 has been taken.

Accordingly, only one element will be studied in this chapter: the cleanup of the debris. Ground Zero was undoubtedly a crime scene and therefore the removal of the debris should not have been standard. There is a protocol to follow for proper investigation to take place. The City of New York did not respect this protocol and began collecting and recycling rubble without delay, meaning that any evidence disappeared with it. By September 28, 2001, even before the start of any investigation, almost 130,000 tons had already been removed. Concerning the steel, David Griffin stated that it was sold:

> to scrap dealers and exported to other countries, such as China and Korea. This fact is possibly significant because, if explosives had been used to break the steel columns, these columns would have had tell-tale signs of the impact of these explosives. Generally, removing any evidence from the scene of a crime is a federal offense. But in this case, the FBI allowed this removal to go forward.[203]

It was confirmed by Architects & Engineers for 9/11 Truth, an organization consisting of 3,000 architects and civil engineers. Quoting Article 205, § 205.50, of the New York Penal Code— Hindering Prosecution:

> [...] a person 'renders criminal assistance' when, with intent to prevent, hinder or delay the discovery or apprehension of [...] a person he knows or believes has committed a crime, [...] he...suppresses, by any act of concealment, alteration or destruction, any physical evidence which might aid in the

---

203. *The 9/11 Commission Report – Omissions and Distortions*, David Ray Griffin, p. 30.

discovery or apprehension of such person or in the lodging of a criminal charge against him.[204]

This penal article could also apply to the disappearance of the black boxes, for which FBI agents could be responsible (it will be addressed below). The FBI let evidence vanish, including trusses and internal support columns, despite protests by experts, the *New York Times*, families of victims, and others. Nothing ever stopped nor even slowed the pace of operations.

The official excuse was that steel should be removed quickly to save survivors trapped in the ruins. Of course, this is a valid reason, but as David Griffin notes:

> This excuse, however, brings up another reason why focusing on the collapse of Building 7 is especially important: Everyone had been evacuated from the building many hours before it collapsed at about 5:30 pm, so there would have been no victims hidden in the rubble. And yet the steel from Building 7 was removed just as quickly.[205]

Even Larry Silverstein—when he used the verb "to pull"—confirmed that a controlled demolition was triggered with explosives, of which traces could normally have been found. However, major questions were left unanswered: when, by whom and to what end were they put in Building 7, and possibly the Twin Towers?

Finally, US Congressman Joseph Crowley, 7th District, New York, declared on the rubble:

There is so much that has been lost in these last six months

---

204. *Documenting the Destruction of Physical Evidence at the World Trade Center*, Ted Walter, Tony Szamboti, and Dennis McMahon, Architects & Engineers for 9/11 Truth, April 11, 2018.
205. *The 9/11 Commission Report – Omissions and Distortions*, David Ray Griffin, p. 30.

that we can never go back and retrieve. And that is not only unfortunate, it is borderline criminal.[206]

Just "borderline"?

The Mysterious Black Boxes of 9/11

Airliners are equipped with two "black boxes," that are in fact orange. They are almost indestructible, shockproof and able to resist to high-intensity fires over 1,100° C for one hour, which is the combustion temperature of kerosene and much hotter than in the WTC. They contain two parts:
 – the Flight Data Recorder (FDR), which records dozens of parameters collected several times per second, like altitude, speed, trajectory, etc.,
 – and the Cockpit Voice Recorder (CVR), which records the audio environment on the flight deck.

According to the FBI and the Commission, none of the four black boxes (flights AA11 and UA175) were recovered in the World Trade Center rubble.[207] Is it surprising that the boxes got lost considering how quickly the debris was removed? After all, recovering a terrorist's intact passport posed no problems, as proven by the FBI (see next chapter), but ultra-solid black boxes could not be found. Yet, the 9/11 Consensus Panel, which groups independent experts[208], reports:

> The official claims above are contradicted by a substantial amount of evidence to the contrary:
> – Contrary to the official claim about AA11 and UA175, a

---

206. *Documenting the Destruction of Physical Evidence at the World Trade Center*, Ted Walter, Tony Szamboti, and Dennis McMahon, Architects & Engineers for 9/11 Truth, April 11, 2018.
207. *9/11 Commission Report*, p. 456, note 76.
208. www.consensus911.org

FDNY fireman who worked in the cleanup of Ground Zero, Nicholas DeMasi, and volunteer Mike Bellone, described their discovery in October 2001 of three of the four black boxes in the rubble of the Twin Towers.[8]

– A September 18, 2001, memorandum to Governor George Pataki from New York State Emergency Management Office Director Edward F. Jacoby, Jr., reported that "Investigators have identified the signal from one of the black boxes in the WTC debris."[9]

– Gen. Paul Kern, the commanding general of the U.S. Army Materiel Command, reported in 2002 that "Radio frequency detectors developed at CECOM [Communications Electronics Command] were used to find "black box" flight recorders from the airliners that crashed into the two towers."[10][209]

Nicholas DeMasi and Michael Bellone's story is further detailed in an article by Pulitzer Prize recipient William Bunch, taken from *Behind-the-Scenes: Ground* Zero[210] and published in *Philadelphia News* on October 28, 2004:

Two men who worked extensively in the wreckage of the World Trade Center claim they helped federal agents find three of the

209. *Point Flt-4: Unexplained Black Box Anomalies for the Four 9/11 Planes*, Consensus 9/11. Notes:

[8] Gail Swanson and Robert Nahas, eds., "Behind-the-scenes: Ground Zero … A Collection of Personal Accounts" (2003); Will Bunch, "New Coverup Revealed? 9/11 Black Boxes Found," *Philadelphia News*, October 28, 2004. [9] Edward F. Jacoby, Jr., "Sept. 18, 2001, memo to Gov. George Pataki." OEM FOIL Sec. 4, p. 16. Edward Jacobi was the director of the New York State Emergency Management Office, responsible for marshaling 22 state agencies and nearly 17,000 personnel, including 5,200 National Guardsmen and 500 state police officers. [10] General Paul J. Kern, "AMC: Accelerating the Pace of Transformation," *AUSA: Army Magazine*, February 1, 2002. Kern headed the US Army Materiel Command from October 2001 to November 2004, *Wikipedia*, (accessed August 30, 2014).

210. *Behind-the-Scenes: Ground Zero*, de Gail Swanson, avec l'Honorary Firefighter Mike Bellone et le pompier retraité Robert Barrett, TRAC Team, 2003.

four "black boxes" from the jetliners that struck the towers on 9/11—contradicting the official account. [...]

DeMasi, an all-terrain vehicles hobbyist, said he donated 4 ATVs to the clean-up and became known as "the ATV Guy."

"At one point, I was asked to take Federal Agents around the site to search for the black boxes from the planes," he wrote. "We were getting ready to go out. My ATV was parked at the top of the stairs at the Brooks Brothers entrance area. We loaded up about a million dollars worth of equipment and strapped it into the ATV..."

"There were a total of four black boxes. We found three."

Efforts over several days to locate and interview DeMasi, who is now said to be with the FDNY's Marine Unit, were not successful.[211]

His account completely contradicts government version, but was corroborated by recovery site volunteer Bellone, as William Bunch recounts:

[Mr Bellone] recalled FBI agents arriving for the search one day in early October, setting up their equipment near Brooks Brothers. He said he didn't go out with them on the ATV but observed their search.

At one point, Bellone said he observed the team with a box that appeared charred but was redish-orange with two white stripes. Pictures of the flight recorders on the NTSB and other Web sites show devices that are orange, with two white stripes.

"There was the one that I saw, and two others were recovered in different locations—but I wasn't there for the other two," Bellone said. He said the FBI agents left with the boxes.

---

211. *New Cover-up revealed? 9/11 Black Boxes found*, William Bunch, *Philadelphia News*, 28 October 2004.

If the account by DeMasi and Bellone is true, it's not clear what motive federal authorities would have for claiming they weren't found.

By the same token, however, it's not clear what incentive either man would have to lie.[212]

It would have been interesting if the *New York Times* had further questioned Bellone, who is known by its journalists. He was interviewed at least twice in 2002, on March 24 and June 15, with articles signed by Tina Kelley and Constance L. Hays. It is, however, possible that he had been solicited but refused, because his statement was already of importance and he wanted to avoid exposing himself by accusing the FBI of lying. Without concrete proof, he would not have been able to withstand the ensuing storm. Nevertheless, new information was published in 2016:

> As well as denying that the black boxes were found, government officials instructed witnesses to keep quiet about the discoveries, according to Mike Bellone. Bellone said he "had a visit from an FBI agent that said I shouldn't discuss the matter" of the recovery of the black boxes. When he asked why he should keep quiet, the agent told him: "It's something that we really shouldn't discuss right now. You really shouldn't talk about it." [...]
> And yet this behavior appears to make no sense. Dave Lindorff commented: "Why would the main intelligence and law enforcement arm of the U.S. government want to hide from the public not just the available information about the two hijacked flights that provided the motivation and justification for the nation's 'war on terror,' and for its two wars against Afghanistan and Iraq, but even the fact that it has the

212. *New Cover-up revealed? 9/11 Black Boxes found*, by Will Bunch, *Philadelphia News*, 28 October 2004.

devices which could contain that information?"[24] In other words, why would the government suppress information that should have strengthened its case for fighting the "war on terror"?[24][213]

It is, indeed, a good question, but we should not expect any answers from the FBI. William Bunch continues his black box article in the following manner:

"It's extremely rare that we don't get the recorders back. I can't recall another domestic case in which we did not recover the recorders," Ted Lopatkiewicz, spokesman for the National Transportation Safety Board, told CBS News in 2002.

That being said, a "domestic case" of this magnitude had never happened before. But, another piece of information further corroborated the statements of Nicholas DeMasi and Michael Bellone:

In an attempt to learn what happened to the black boxes from the planes that hit the Twin Towers, investigative reporter Dave Lindorff talked to someone from the National Transportation Safety Board (NTSB)—the government agency that is responsible for investigating every civil aviation accident that occurs in the United States. Lindorff asked, "How many of these boxes did they actually ever find?" The NTSB official asked Lindorff if he wanted "the real answer or the official answer." Lindorff said he wanted the real answer and was told,

213. 9/11 Black Boxes From WTC Plane Strikes Recovered By Rescuers, Authorities Covered This Up, Shoestring, Portland Independant Media Center, 6 September 2006, http://portland.indymedia.org/en/2016/09/433089.shtml. Note [24]: Dave Lindorff, 9/11: Missing Black Boxes in World Trade Center Attacks Found by Firefighters, Analyzed by NTSB, Concealed by FBI.

"Well then, that has to be off the record." The official then said, "We got all four of them and ... they're now in the possession of the FBI, which took them away from us."[214]

If the FBI indeed confiscated the black boxes like it did the Washington tapes, we would have the explanation for this unique domestic case in which they were not found. However, discovering that the government agency in charge of the investigation and law enforcement hid vital evidence would be distressing to say the least. What did they have to hide?

Note that both of AA77's black boxes were found at the Pentagon, but not without inconsistencies (which will be detailed in Chapter *9/11 The FBI Lies*).

The House of Saud Takes Off

At 10:57 a.m. the FAA confirmed a ban on all commercial and private flights on national territory. Surprisingly, the only authorized flights transported Saudis, especially members of the bin Laden family who were being exfiltrated from the United States. On p. 13 of *House of Bush, House of Saud* (*Chapter 1 – The Great Escape*) Craig Unger writes:

> A global manhunt of unprecedented proportions was under way. Thousands of people had just been killed by Osama bin Laden. Didn't it make sense to at least interview his relatives and other Saudis who, inadvertently or not, may have aided him?
>
> Moreover, Attorney General John Ashcroft had asserted that the government "had a responsibility to use every legal means

---

214. *9/11 Black Boxes From WTC Plane Strikes Recovered By Rescuers, Authorities Covered This Up*, Shoestring, Portland Independant Media Center, 6 September 2006, http://portland.indymedia.org/en/2016/09/433089.shtml.

at our disposal to prevent further terrorist activity by taking people into custody who have violated the law and who may pose a threat to America." All over the country Arabs were being rounded up and interrogated. By the weekend after the attacks, Ashcroft, to the dismay of civil libertarians, had already put together a package of proposals broadening the FBI's power to detain foreigners, wiretap them, and trace money laundering to terrorists. Some suspects would be held for as long as ten months at the American naval base in Guantanamo, Cuba.

In an ordinary murder investigation, it is commonplace to interview relatives of the prime suspect. [...] How did the Saudis get a pass?

And did a simple disclaimer from the bin Laden family mean no one in the entire family had any contacts or useful information whatsoever? Did that mean the FBI should simply drop all further inquiries? At the very least, wouldn't family members be able to provide U.S. investigators with some information about Osama's finances, people who might know who him or might be aiding Al Qaeda?[215]

Could this happen without the FBI's knowledge? Impossible, as confirmed by Richard Clarke:

"Somebody brought to us for approval the decision to let an airplane filled with Saudis, including members of the bin Laden family, leave the country", Clarke says. "My role was to say that it can't happen until the FBI approves it. And so the FBI was asked—we had a live connection to the FBI—and we asked the FBI to make sure that they were satisfied that everybody getting on that plane was someone that it was O.K.

---

215. *House of Bush, House of Saud*, Craig Unger, Gibson Square, London, 2007, p. 13.

to leave. And they came back and said yes, it was fine with them. So we said, "Fine, let it happen."[216]

Unsurprisingly, when the story started to make headlines:

Officially, the FBI says it had nothing to do with the repatriation of the Saudis. "I can say unequivocally that the FBI had no role in facilitating these flights one way or another," says Special Agent John Iannarelli.[217]

Thus we are asked to believe that "the FBI had no role in facilitating these flights one way or another." A flight ban was in place, and yet planes of Saudis, including bin Ladens, could slip quietly out of American airspace unopposed.

Unfortunately for the Bureau, the facts were quickly restored when Prince Bandar bin Sultan, Ambassador of Saudi Arabia in Washington, stated to CNN:

With coordination with the FBI, we got them all out.[218]

Pay attention to the word "coordination." Such an evacuation could not have happened without clearance from upper-echelon FBI members, and the State Department at the very least. In other words, the FBI did not find it necessary to question the bin Ladens and other Saudis fleeing the country after 9/11. Strange, isn't it?

---

216. *House of Bush, House of Saud*, Craig Unger, p. 253.
217. *House of Bush, House of Saud*, Craig Unger, p. 10.
218. *House of Bush, House of Saud*, Craig Unger, p. 10.

Embarrassing Suspects and Witnesses?

If we were to believe the government conspiracy narrative, FBI behavior towards the Saudis was bewildering. And not only in the context of the aforementioned flights. For example:

> The 9/11 Congressional Inquiry's final report concludes that at least six hijackers received "substantial assistance" from associates in the U.S., though it is "not known to what extent any of these contacts in the United States were aware of the plot." These hijackers came into contact with at least 14 people who were investigated by the FBI before 9/11, and four of these investigations were active while the hijackers were present.
> [...] Other contacts provided legal, logistical, or financial assistance, facilitated U.S. entry and flight school enrollment, or were known from [al-Qaeda]-related activities or training. (9/11 Congressional Inquiry, 7/24/2003).[219]

Nine people are then identified, but:

> None of the above figures have been arrested or even publicly charged of any terrorist crime.

This is puzzling. One could ask what use the FBI is if it does not interrogate terrorist accomplices. The case of Omar al-Bayoumi is particularly disturbing as David Griffin sums up:

> In 1999, while living in San Diego, he picked up two of the (alleged) hijackers-Nawaf Alhazmi and Khalid Almihdhar-at the Los Angeles airport, set them up in an apartment near his place, and helped them locate flight schools. He was thought by an FBI informer to be a Saudi intelligence officer. After

219. *The Terror Timeline*, p. 527-8.

9/11, he was arrested by agents in England, where he had moved two months earlier; but the FBI, saying that it believed his story that he had met Nawaf Alhazmi and Khalid Almihdhar by chance, had him released.

[…] In spite of all this evidence, however, the FBI closed its case on al-Bayoumi, claiming that he had only "briefly lent money to two of the 19 hijackers" and that all his assistance to them was "in compliance with the Muslim custom of being kind to strangers [rather] than out of some relationship with Saudi Intelligence."[220]

This is a far-fetched excuse when one looks at the available evidence, among which help given to the pair of terrorists and multiple exchanges with Saudi authorities. All the more as, in August 2002, the CIA labeled him as an "agent" with

incontrovertible evidence that there is support for these terrorists [among them al-Bayoumi] within the Saudi government.[221]

The conclusion of the al-Bayoumi FBI report stunned Senator Bob Graham, who co-presided over the investigation by Congress on 9/11. He

asked to interview the FBI agents who made this report, but FBI Director Robert Mueller refused to allow this.[222]

Robert Mueller's name is showing up in all the right places, it seems. Why did he refuse? What risk is there in a senator questioning agents?

---

220. *The 9/11 Commission Report – Omissions and Distortions*, p. 68.
221. *Intelligence Matters: The CIA, the FBI, Saudi Arabia, and the Failure of America's War on Terror*, Bob Graham, Random House, 2004, p. 169, quoted in *The 9/11 Commission Report – Omissions and Distortions*, p. 68.
222. *The 9/11 Commission Report – Omissions and Distortions*, p. 68.

Possibly even more mystifying is how the FBI handled another case involving the two San Diego based terrorists:

> October 5, 2002: FBI Refuses to Allow FBI Informant
> to Testify Before 9/11 Inquiry
> *The New York Times* reports that the FBI is refusing to allow Abdussattar Shaikh, the FBI informant who lived with hijackers Nawaf Alhazmi and Khalid Almihdhar in the second half of 2000, to testify before the 9/11 Congressional Inquiry. The FBI claims the informer would have nothing interesting to say. The Justice Department also wants to learn more about the informant. (*New York Times*, 10/5/02).
> The FBI also tries to prevent Shaikh's handler Steven Butler from testifying, but Butler does end up testifying before a secret session on October 9, 2002. Shaikh does not testify at all. (*Washington* Post, 10/11/02).[223]

Senator Graham came forward with new information on the Shaikh case, which raised further questions FBI's involvement in 9/11:

> "He was an informant for the FBI, as a paid asset," Graham said. "His principle responsibility was monitoring Saudi youth living in the San Diego community as to whether they were contemplating any actions that would be detrimental to the United States."
> The former senator said his staffers were never able to to interview him.
> "He was taken into protective custody immediately after 9/11 and held for the better part of four years, at the end of which he was given a $100,000 payment and discharged of his responsibilities," Graham said. "He was withheld from us and

---

223. *The Terror Timeline*, p. 516.

in my own opinion, it was purposeful so that we would not get access to whatever information he had."[224]

What did the FBI want to hide in protecting these individuals and other terrorist accomplices? This is no longer a question of "failure" and "incompetency," which we do not believe for a second. Instead, a more distressing scenario appears, a plan through which the FBI tried to prove the government conspiracy narrative—no matter the cost.

The FBI, Guardian of the House of Saud

For Bob Graham, it is as if the FBI's actions seek to clear the Saudis of any involvement. In fact, it seems increasingly likely that Saudi Arabia was one of the main actors, which is exactly what the FBI would be attempting to hide. Why? What would be in it for the FBI? How could one believe this monarchy to have been the brains or sponsors behind 9/11, despite tarnishing the very concept of humanity through its support of terrorism, the war in Yemen, violent interventions in Bahrain, etc.? If it were the case, it would require less than a day, not even twelve minutes for the US to overthrow them. In fact, it had no reason to launch such an attack on the very guardian who had been watching over Saudi Arabia since the 1945 Quincy Agreement, which would have been renewed in 2005 for another sixty years. The monarchy knows that its American protector has control over their life and death, even if President Barack Obama received heavy criticism for the way he bowed to King Abdallah.[225]

Once again, the question of interest arises; it is yet to be determined what the Bureau could gain from this.

However, for the government version of the conspiracy to thrive

---

224. *Questions Linger Over San Diego 9/11 Hijackers' Ties to Saudi Government*, Amita Sharma, KPBS, September 7, 2011.
225. See, for example, the photo in *Barack Obama criticised for 'bowing' to King Abdullah of Saudi Arabia*, Alex Spillius, *The Telegraph*, April 8, 2009.

and hide the real culprits, it is vital that the people believe in the involvement of Muslims with foreign financial support, logistics, etc. Although the designated "kamikazes" were unable to pilot airliners or even carry out such a complex military operation, this raised no concern as the investigation would inevitably be entrusted to the FBI, the director of which had been appointed by President Bush a week before the events. Who else would they turn to but the Saudis, who could not refuse, and the allied Pakistani ISI intelligence agency, who also contributed?

How else should we interpret the decisions made by the Bush and Obama administrations? They did everything in their power to prevent the monarchy from being prosecuted by victims' families, including classifying the famous "twenty-eight pages."

Not having done so could make it too obvious that the kingdom, as much as bin Laden and the other convicted terrorists, were mere puppets. The true sponsors and orchestrators pulling the strings would finally be brought to light, with immeasurable consequences for the USA and the world. Such consequences would not pardon the FBI from what is increasingly looking like complicity. It does not exclude another (allied) country from being involved either.

"President George W. Bush meets with Saudi Arabian Ambassador Prince Bandar bin Sultan at the Bush Ranch in Crawford, Texas (27 August, 2002)."
The royal family, of which this eminent prince is familiar with G. W. Bush, allegedly perpetrated 9/11?
Who could believe such a story?

Chapter 9/9

The FBI Forged False Evidence?

An investigative agency should be expected to have a pristine record at all levels. Thus far it has been difficult to suggest that the FBI lived up to this rule, at least for the 9/11 investigation. This chapter could further worsen things as it should be pondered whether the FBI fabricated evidence, which Chapter 6 – *The FBI Silenced* introduced. Such actions would constitute a federal crime, and confirm 9/11 complicity. Then the FBI's "contribution" would have been to foe the world by hiding the true culprits. It is difficult to imagine what would follow if these facts turned out to be true.

Overly Catholic Muslims

In Chapter 4 of *9/11 The Big Lie* titled *The FBI Wrings its Hands*, Thierry Meyssan reports that the Muslim kamikaze theory was confirmed by the FBI after the discover of documents handwritten in Arabic:

> Three copies were said to have been found: one in a suitcase that was lost in transit between flights, belonging to Mohammed Atta; the second in a vehicle abandoned at Dulles Airport by Nawaf Al-Hazmi and the third among the debris of flight 93 which exploded over Stony Creek Township, Pennsylvania.[42]

> Note 42: Several European newspapers mistakenly indicated that the FBI had discovered this document in the ruins at the Pentagon.[226]

---

226. *9/11 The Big Lie*, p. 52.

The FBI published an English translation that was taken up by the media.[227] It consists of five pages of pious guidelines:

> 1) Recite the pledge you have taken to die and renew your intention. Shave your body and anoint it with eau de Cologne. Take a shower.
> 2) Make sure you are completely familiar with all the details of the plan and prepare yourself for an eventual riposte or reaction from the enemy.
> 3) Read Al-Tawba and Anfal [martial Suras or chapters from the Koran], reflect on their meaning and think of all that God has promised to martyrs."
> Etc.

In *The Guardian*, Anne Karpf was surprised that one of the pieces of advice given included "to shine your shoes before you meet your maker."[228] This is undoubtedly vital.

The *Independent* noticed further dubious contents:

> The "note suggests an almost Christian view of what the hijackers might have felt" and is filled with "weird" comments that Muslims would never say, such as "the time of fun and waste is gone." If the note "is genuine, then the [hijackers] believed in a very exclusive version of Islam—or were surprisingly unfamiliar with their religion." (*Independent*, 9/29/01).[229]

Thierry Meyssan makes a similar observation:

---

227. Note 41 in *9/11 The Big Lie* on this document: Briefing by the Attorney General, John Ashcroft, and the FBI director, Robert Mueller III, 28 September 2001, http://www.usdoj.gov/ag/agcrisisremarks9_28.htm
228. *Uncle Sam's Lucky Finds*, Anne Karpf, *TheGuardian*, 19 March 2002.
229. *The Terror Timeline*, p. 502.

Written in a classic theological style, often full of medieval references, these documents greatly contributed to feeding the image of fanatics that the American authorities exposed to popular wrath. Nevertheless, they were crude forgeries, whose incongruities would have been spotted by any person knowledgeable about Islam. For instance, they begin with the exhortation, "In the name of God, of myself and of my family" (sic), whereas Muslims—as opposed to numerous puritan sects in America—never pray in their own name, or that of their family.[43] Similarly, the text includes in one phrase an Americanism which has no place in vocabulary derived from the Koran: "You must face it and understand it 100%."[230]

In footnote 43, Thierry Meyssan states that:

Curiously, the star reporter Bob Woodward pointed out this anomaly on the day it was published, but did not derive any conclusions. See *In Hijacker's Bags, a Call to Planning, Prayer and Death*, *Washington Post*, 28 September 2001, http://www.washingtonpost.com.

The "100%" theme is, indeed, not very Koranic. In fact, this document seems "100%" fake. Is it for this reason that FBI Director Robert Mueller declared the following on April 19, 2002, during a conference at the Commonwealth Club of California, in San Francisco:

The hijackers also left no paper trail. In our investigation, we have not uncovered a single piece of paper—either here in the U.S. or in the treasure trove of information that has turned up in Afghanistan and elsewhere—that mentioned any aspect of the September 11th plot.[231]

---

230. *9/11 The Big Lie*, p. 52.
231. https://archives.fbi.gov/archives/news/speeches/partnership-and-preven-tion-the-fbis-role-in-homeland-security

"No paper trail"? Either he lied during the conference, or when the English translation of the text was presented in 2001. The third possibility is that he had thought the document to be real, before learning that it was a fake and thus not revealing it. If we stick to his statement in San Francisco, the 2001 document "discovered" by his agents was necessarily a forgery. As director, he must have taken punitive action against the guilty parties under his authority for such a crime, although the lack of an official announcement.

Despite "the treasure trove of information," if not a single "aspect of the September 11th plot" was mentioned, we can once more ask whether the nineteen officially designated hijackers really perpetrated 9/11. Luckily for the FBI, Robert Mueller anticipated this pitfall and added the following:

> What emerged from our massive investigation was a sobering portrait of 19 hijackers who carried out their attacks with meticulous planning, extraordinary secrecy, and extensive knowledge of how America works.
>
> The plans were hatched and financed overseas, beginning as long as five years ago. [...]
>
> While here, the hijackers did all they could to stay below our radar. They contacted no known terrorist sympathizers. They committed no egregious crimes. They dressed and acted like Americans, shopping and eating at places like Wal-Mart and Pizza Hut, blending into the woodwork all the while. When four got speeding tickets in the days leading up to September 11th, they remained calm and aroused no suspicion. Since none were known terrorists, law enforcement had no reason to question or detain them.
>
> [...] The hijackers had no computers, no laptops, no storage media of any kind. They used hundreds of different pay phones and cell phones, often with prepaid calling cards that are extremely difficult to trace. And they made sure that all the

money sent to them to fund their attacks was wired in small amounts to avoid detection.

In short, the terrorists had managed to exploit loopholes and vulnerabilities in our systems, to stay out of sight, and to not let anyone know what they were up to beyond a very closed circle.

For a "very closed circle" it contained FBI agents as demonstrated in previous chapters. The declaration sounds dishonest, including the hijacker profiles that he presented. One only needs to read *The Terror Timeline* to be assured of the opposite. For example, on p. 191:

> June 2000: Hijackers Open Many Bank Accounts
> in Florida; Transactions Not Followed
> Mohamed Atta and other hijackers begin to open bank accounts in Florida. At least 35 accounts are opened, 14 of them at Sun Trust Bank. All are opened with fake social security numbers (some with randomly made up numbers), yet none of the accounts are checked or questioned by the banks. (*New York Times*, 7/10/02). One transfer from the United Arab Emirates three months later totaling $69,985 prompts the bank to make a "suspicious transaction report" to the U.S. Treasury's Financial Crimes Enforcement Network. Apparently, no investigation into this transaction occurs. (*Financial Times*, 11/29/01).

Similarly, according to Mueller, the terrorists had no laptops. Yet, FBI headquarters tampered with the Minneapolis search warrant for none other than Moussaoui's laptop, among so many examples. How could Director Mueller still be credible after such statements?

It does not end there, as the Arabic document is not the only one whith questionable authenticity.

Indestructible Passports

If 9/11 not had not been such a tragedy, this would rank among the most ridiculous fallacies announced by the FBI and spread by the media.

During the Public Hearing on January 26, 2004, at the National Commission on Terrorist Attacks Upon the United States, in the Senate, Susan Ginsburg, "who directs the part of the investigation that pertains to the subject of today's hearing," declared:

> Beginning with passports. Four of the hijackers passports have survived in whole or in part. Two were recovered from the crash site of United Airlines flight 93 in Pennsylvania. These are the passports of Ziad Jarrah and Saeed al Ghamdi. One belonged to a hijacker on American Airlines flight 11. This is the passport of Satam al Suqami. A passerby picked it up and gave it to a NYPD detective shortly before the World Trade Center towers collapsed. A fourth passport was recovered from luggage that did not make it from a Portland flight to Boston on to the connecting flight which was American Airlines flight 11. This is the passport of Abdul Aziz al Omari.[232]

The last fact will be addressed first, as it offers little interest for the overall study. Beyond the fact that passengers would carry their passports with them, how could the terrorist have boarded a flight without it in the first place? Did he carry another one under the same name? The third case is more intriguing.

The public story on the passport's discovery emerged on September 18, 2001. Barry Mawn, director of New York's FBI office, explained that:

> Police and the FBI completed a grid search of area streets

---

232. http://www.9-11commission.gov/archive/hearing7/9-11Commission_Hearing_2004-01-26.htm

near the site of the World Trade Center looking for clues, […]. The searchers found several clues, he said, but would not elaborate. Last week, a passport belonging to one of the hijackers was found in the vicinity of Vesey Street, near the World Trade Center. "It was a significant piece of evidence for us," Mawn said.[233]

It was Satam al Suqami's passport—not Mohammed Atta's as initially announced by some authors—one of the terrorists on Flight AA11 that crashed into North Tower. A map of the zone shows that Vesey Street is located on the side that was hit. It would have required a miracle for the passport to fly over an entire block, but it remains possible all things considered.

However, if we watch the crash filmed by the Naudet brothers, how could the passport have dropped from the plane and flown away? It would have had to escape from the plane precisely on impact before the near-immediate ignition of the fire engulfed it in flames. Satam al Suqami certainly did not have the passport in his hand, unless he had somehow found an ingenious way to weaponize it. Logic dictates that it was in his jacket or bag, from which it would have taken powers beyond our understanding to extract the flimsy document. Should this not be the case, a paper booklet not only resisted steel-bending fire, but also the tower's collapse, before landing in Vesey Street. This is where one should draw the line in terms of possibility.

It is astonishing that New York's FBI office director was not surprised by this and simply declared "It was a significant piece of evidence for us." Is the sheer probability of the FBI recovering a passport in such a manner not inexistent? Add to this the fact that the passport was unscathed and that of a hijacker—not a crew member or passenger—and a preposterous scenario emerges.

---

233. *Ashcroft says more attacks may be planned*, CNN Correspondents Kelli Arena, Susan Candiotti and Eileen O'Connor, CNN, September 18, 2001.

Anne Karpf justly remarked:

> [T]he idea that [this] passport had escaped from that inferno unsinged would [test] the credulity of the staunchest supporter of the FBI's crackdown on terrorism.[234]

In fact, it was so improbable that Susan Ginsburg's January 2004 version had been modified from the initial FBI version: it was no longer discovered by an agent but "a passerby picked it up and gave it to a NYPD detective shortly before the World Trade Center towers collapsed." Even if it did not have to survive the collapse of the WTC, this story is not any less far-fetched. Is "a significant piece of evidence" fabricated by the FBI not closer to the truth? Did they seek to convince the world that Muslim fanatics perpetrated 9/11?

Indestructible Passports, continued

Susan Ginsburg and the Commission also said that the passports of Ziad Jarrah and Saeed al Ghamdi were uncovered on the crash site of Flight UA93 in Pennsylvania. Ziad Jarrah was the Lebanese man with an apparent double, whose family had offered DNA fragments to the FBI, that subsequently refused (Chapter 9/6 – The FBI Silenced). Here is what David Griffin had to say:

> Equally absurd is the claim that the passport of Ziad Jarrah, the alleged pilot of Flight 93, was found at this plane's crash site in Pennsylvania.[56] This passport was reportedly found on the ground even though there was virtually nothing at the site to indicate that an airliner had crashed there. The reason for this absence of wreckage, we were told, was that the plane had been headed downward at 580 miles per hour and, when it hit the spongy Pennsylvania soil, buried itself deep in the ground.

---

234. Uncle Sam's Lucky Finds, Anne Karpf, TheGuardian, March 19, 2002.

New York Times journalist Jere Longman, surely repeating what he had been told by authorities, wrote: "The fuselage accordioned on itself more than thirty feet into the porous, backfilled ground. It was as if a marble had been dropped into water."[57] So, we are to believe, just before the plane buried itself in the earth, Jarrah's passport escaped from the cockpit and landed on the ground. Did Jarrah, going 580 miles per hour, have the window open?[58, 235]

Like in New York, how the passport could have ejected itself from the plane is a mystery. The statement also applies to Saeed al Ghamdi's passport, as highlighted by Susan Ginsburg. Again, was the "evidence" presented by the FBI believable?

ID Cards Too!
Footnote 58 at the end of the previous quote from David Griffin's article, *Was America Attacked by Muslims on 9/11?,* details the following:

> In light of the absurdity of the claims about the passports of al-Suqami and Jarrah, we can safely assume that the ID cards of Majed Moqed, Nawaf al-Hazmi, and Salem al-Hazmi, said to have been discovered at the Pentagon crash site [...], were also planted.

The information is taken from a report titled *9/11 And Terrorist Travel*, written by the Commission's team and stating on page 27:

235. Notes 56 and 57 quoted by David Ray Griffin in *Was America Attacked by Muslims on 9/11?*:
56. Sheila MacVicar and Caroline Faraj, "September 11 Hijacker Questioned in January 2001," CNN, 1 August 2002 (http://archives.cnn.com/2002/US/08/01/cia.hijacker/index.html); 9/11 Commission Hearing, 26 January 2004.
57. 9/11CR 14; Jere Longman, *Among the Heroes: United 93 and the Passengers and Crew Who Fought Back* (New York: HarperCollins, 2002), 215.
58. See next paragraph.

The Hazmi brothers' identifications were found in the rubble at the Pentagon and appeared genuine upon examination.[236]

What a stroke of luck it was that they "appeared genuine upon examination." Did the Commission doubt the FBI's integrity?

A False Business Card for the Moussaoui Trial?

The Terror Timeline states on page 224, under the title *September 24, 2002: Discovered Business Card Helps Case Against Moussaoui*, that

> Federal prosecutors say a business card found in the wreckage of Flight 93 provides a link between alleged conspirator Zacarias Moussaoui and hijacker Ziad Jarrah. Supposedly a business card belonging to Jarrah has a phone number written on it, and Moussaoui had once called that number. It was not explained what the number is, whose phone number it was, when Moussaoui called it, when the card was found, or how investigators know the card belonged to Jarrah. (MSNBC, 9/24/02). Interestingly, this find comes just as the case against Moussaoui is facing trouble. For instance, one month earlier, *USA Today* reported that investigators had found no link between Moussaoui and the other hijackers (*USA Today*, 8/29/02).

No comment is necessary. This statement leads to the conclusion that the FBI could fabricate evidence to sentence a man to capital punishment as requested by the prosecutors. Who could believe it?

---

236. *9/11 And Terrorist Travel*, Staff Report of the National Commission on Terrorist Attacks Upon the United States, by Thomas R. Eldridge, Susan Ginsburg, Walter T. Hempel II, Janice L. Kephart, Kelly Moore and Joanne M. Accolla, Staff Assistant, Alice Falk, Editor, August 21, 2004.

Chapter 9/10

The FBI Lost the Money

Hide Those Billions, I Can't Bear Them!

This is one of the essential points in understanding 9/11 and unmasking the culprits and the accomplices. In the following days, information about suspiciously large stock market transactions was published. These had been done by speculators seemingly having knowledge of the attacks before they occurred, what is known as insider trading. In particular, a massive trade of put options targeted three sectors: two airlines (American and United), financial groups renting space at the World Trade Center (Morgan Stanley Dean Witter & Co, Bank of America, Salomon Smith Barney, or Merrill Lynch & Co, headquartered near the Twin Towers), and the insurance sector (Marsh & McLennan, Groupe Axa, Swiss Re, Munich Re...), which will have to pay billions in compensation to its clients. Buying put options means speculating on the fall of shares; in other words, these are high risk operations. Moreover, it seems the trading was not unique to the USA, but occurred worldwide:

> The extent of the 9/11-related informed trading was unprecedented. An ABC News Consultant, Jonathan Winer, said, "it's absolutely unprecedented to see cases of insider trading covering the entire world from Japan to the US to North America to Europe."[10] [237]

Consequently, many governments began investigations into

---

237. *Evidence for Informed Trading on the Attacks of September 11*, Kevin Ryan, *Foreign Policy Journal*, November 18, 2010. Note 10: World News Tonight, September, 20, 2001.

possible insider trading related to the terrorist attacks, in Belgium, Cyprus, France, Germany, Italy, Japan, Luxembourg, Monaco, the Netherlands, Singapore, Switzerland, the United States, etc.

> If successful in tracking the perpetrators [of inside trading], authorities would not only be successful in implicating obvious accomplices in the 9-11 attacks, but also would be able to strike deeply into the infrastructure of a shadow financial network and hundreds of billions of dollars that flow through it.[238]

But, although compelling evidence was piling up, none of the investigations resulted in a single indictment. The Commission dealt, or rather "did away," with this key element through two sentences in Chapter 5 of the *Report*, pp. 171-72:

> There also have been claims that al Qaeda financed itself through manipulation of the stock market based on its advance knowledge of the 9/11 attacks. Exhaustive investigations by the Securities and Exchange Commission, FBI, and other agencies have uncovered no evidence that anyone with advance knowledge of the attacks profited through securities transactions.[130]

And that was that. Footnote N° 130 is a little longer and explains:

> 130. Highly publicized allegations of insider trading in advance of 9/11 generally rest on reports of unusual pre-9/11 trading activity in companies whose stock plummeted after the attacks. Some unusual trading did in fact occur, but each such trade proved to have an innocuous explanation. For

---

238. *Massive pre-attack 'insider trading' offer authorities hottest trail to accomplices*, Kyle F. Hence, globalresearch.ca, April 21, 2002.

example, the volume of put options—investments that pay off only when a stock drops in price—surged in the parent companies of United Airlines on September 6 and American Airlines on September 10—highly suspicious trading on its face. Yet, further investigation has revealed that the trading had no connection with 9/11. A single U.S.-based institutional investor with no conceivable ties to al Qaeda purchased 95 percent of the UAL puts on September 6 as part of a trading strategy that also included buying 115,000 shares of American on September 10. Similarly, much of the seemingly suspicious trading in American on September 10 was traced to a specific U.S.-based options trading newsletter, faxed to its subscribers on Sunday, September 9, which recommended these trades. These examples typify the evidence examined by the investigation. The SEC and the FBI, aided by other agencies and the securities industry, devoted enormous resources to investigating this issue, including securing the cooperation of many foreign governments. These investigators have found that the apparently suspicious consistently proved innocuous.[239]

The two sentences in the *Report* are another embodiment of the partiality, if not blatant dishonesty, of the Commission. Allegations did not relate to the fact that al-Qaeda was involved in trading activities, but that massive insider trading occurred with guilty parties yet to be uncovered. The Commission then hid behind the "Securities and Exchange Commission, FBI, and other agencies" and asserted that there had been no insider trading activities. Otherwise put, it confirms that al-Qaeda did not profit from 9/11 on stock markets despite being the only one to know what was about to happen, as stated by the government version of the conspiracy. Moreover, with

---

239. *The 9/11 Commission Report*, p. 499.

the "enormous resources" devoted to this investigation and "the cooperation of many foreign governments," al-Qaeda certainly did not speculate on American Airlines or United Airlines put options. However, is it fitting to talk of an investigation when it arises that:

> Unfortunately, the British regulator, The Financial Services Authority, wrote off its investigation by simply clearing "bin Laden and his henchmen of insider trading."[240]

It is the same type of "argument" that was used by the SEC, the FBI and the Commission: bin Laden did not commit these stock market offences, therefore, they do not exist even though American speculators got richer (at the demise of 3,000 souls). It is a known fact that capitalism's regard for moral values is non-existent, but how degenerate is this system that judges crimes according to the nationality of the accused? No financial investigation had ever had so many victims at its stake. Then again, admitting that American traders got richer because they had advance knowledge of the attacks would completely sink the government version of the conspiracy.

An Inconvenient Truth
Although the SEC and the FBI did not notice anything suspicious,

> "I saw put-call numbers higher than I've ever seen in 10 years of following the markets, particularly the options markets," said John Kinnucan, principal of Broadband Research quoted in *The San Francisco Chronicle*.[241]

---

240. *Evidence for Informed Trading on the Attacks of September 11*, Kevin Ryan, *Foreign Policy Journal*, November 18, 2010.
241. *Massive pre-attack 'insider trading' offer authorities hottest trail to accomplices*, Kyle F. Hence, globalresearch.ca, April 21, 2002.

Here are some examples of put options during the days before 9/11:

– UAL Corp (parent for United Airlines): shot up 285 times the average volume, representing 75 times the total number of put options ever traded up until that time;

– United Airlines: the number of put option contracts soared 90 times the total of the three previous weeks in one day;

– AMR (parent for American Airlines): on September 10, the number of put options reached 60 times the daily average and five times the total of all $30 put options traded before.

Remember that these options are highly speculative and risky: if the shares do not fall, it would constitute a net loss for the speculator. The institutions in charge of protecting the American people—the SEC, the FBI and even the 9/11 Commission—explained that these movements may seem abnormal, but that they were due to a bear market phase. However, as Kyle F. Hence points out:

> Most anomalous were the huge put option trading spikes placed in only two of the three major US airlines. Almost always, if investors believe the airline industry is due to drop, they will short all three major carriers. This was not the case here because Delta did not see spikes similar to UAL and AMR.[242]

Indeed, no similar trading on other airlines occurred on the Chicago exchanges in the days preceding September 11. Here are two similar examples in the finance industry:

> – Morgan Stanley Dean Witter & Co, which occupied 22 floors of the World Trade Center, saw 2,157 of its October $45 put options bought in the three trading days before Black Tuesday; this compares to an average of 27 contracts per day before September 6. [...].

---

242. *Massive pre-attack 'insider trading' offer authorities hottest trail to accomplices*, Kyle F. Hence, globalresearch.ca, April 21, 2002.

– Merrill Lynch & Co, with headquarters near the Twin Towers, saw 12,215 October $45 put options bought in the four trading days before the attacks; the previous average volume in those shares had been 252 contracts per day (a 1,200% increase).[243]

K. Hence added that, even if the media focused on the massive trading of put options, insiders used various financial instruments:

The *Wall Street Journal* reported on October 2 that the Secret Service had begun a probe into an unusually high volume of five-year US Treasury note purchases made prior to the attacks. The Treasury note transactions included a single $5 billion trade. The *Journal* noted that "Five-year Treasury notes are among the best investments in the event of a world crisis, especially one that hits the US. The notes are prized for their safety and their backing by the US government, and usually rally when investors flee riskier investments, such as stocks." The value of these notes, the *Journal* pointed out, has risen sharply after the events of September 11.
[...] German central bank president, Ernst Welteke, said his bank conducted a study that strongly indicated "terrorism insider trading" associated with 9/11. He stated that his researchers had found "almost irrefutable proof of insider trading."[(8)] Welteke suggested that the insider trading occurred not only in shares of companies affected by the attacks, such as airlines and insurance companies, but also in gold and oil.[(9)244]

243. *Insider Trading on 9/11: Speculative Trade in "Put Options". The Financial Facts Laid Bare*, Lars Schall, Global Research, September 17, 2015.
244. *Evidence for Informed Trading on the Attacks of September 11*, Kevin Ryan, *Foreign Policy Journal*, November 18, 2010. Notes:
(8) Paul Thompson and The Center for Cooperative Research, *Terror Timeline: Year by Year, Day by Day, Minute by Minute: A Comprehensive Chronicle of the Road to 9/11 – and America's Response*, Harper Collins, 2004. Also found at History Commons, *Complete 9/11 Timeline, Insider Trading and Other Foreknowledge*http://

But the fraud went further, even rampant:

> According to a Reuters report of December 16, German data retrieval experts, hired by WTC tenant firms, were mining data off damaged hard disks recovered from the ground zero. The goal is to discover who was responsible for the movement of unusually large sums of money through the computers of the WTC in the hours before the attack. Peter Henschel, director of Convar, the firm responsible, said, "not only the volume, but the size of the transactions was far higher than usual for a day like that." Richard Wagner, a data retrieval expert estimated that more than $100 million in illegal transactions appeared to have rushed through the WTC computers before and during the disaster.[245] "They thought that the records of their transactions could not be traced after the main frames were destroyed."[246]

Examples are limitless, especially with work published later by academics such as Marc Chesney, Remo Crameri and Loriano Mancini from the University of Zurich[247], confirming massive insider trading linked to 9/11.

Given the absence of a thorough investigation, it is difficult, if not impossible, to determine the true extent of proceeds from criminal and unscrupulous speculating. Estimates range from hundreds to billions of dollars:

---

www.historycommons.org/timeline.jsp?timeline=complete_911_timeline&before_9/11=insidertrading

(9) Associated Press, *EU Searches for Suspicious Trading* , 22 September 2001, http://www.foxnews.com/story/0,2933,34910,00.html.

245. *Massive pre-attack 'insider trading' offer authorities hottest trail to accomplices*, Kyle F. Hence, globalresearch.ca, April 21, 2002.

246. *Evidence for Informed Trading on the Attacks of September 11*, Kevin Ryan, *Foreign Policy Journal*, November 18, 2010.

247. *Detecting Informed Trading Activities in the Options Markets*, Marc Chesney, Remo Crameri and Loriano Mancini, University of Zurich, September 1, 2009.

According to Phil Erlanger, a former Senior Technical Analyst with Fidelity, and founder of a Florida firm that tracks short selling and options trading, insiders made off with billions (not mere millions) in profits by betting on the fall of stocks they knew would tumble in the aftermath of the WTC and Pentagon attacks.[248]

Andreas von Bülow, a former German minister, believes it could be up to $15 billion.[249] But since bin Laden was not involved, authorities declared it all quiet on the Western Front. Although:

The evidence and comments offered by traders, analysts, bankers and others in the immediate aftermath indicates there was, in fact, a carefully planned and sophisticated effort of massive profiteering from the precipitous fall of stocks that occurred when trading opened following the attack. This is expert documentation and observations based on years of experience. The implications are absolutely frightening. And all the more reason for authorities to pull out all the stops to identify and prosecute those responsible and shut down the global financial network facilitated the most heinous of crimes. Unfortunately, that's not exactly what happened.[250]

However, as Kyle Hence stressed, "a real war on terrorism would lead to seizures of billions not millions."

---

248. *Massive pre-attack 'insider trading' offer authorities hottest trail to accomplices,* Kyle F. Hence, globalresearch.ca, April 21, 2002.
249. *Evidence for Informed Trading on the Attacks of September 11,* Kevin Ryan, *Foreign Policy Journal,* November 18, 2010.
250. *Massive pre-attack 'insider trading' offer authorities hottest trail to accomplices,* Kyle F. Hence, globalresearch.ca, April 21, 2002.

The FBI Beyond All Suspicion?

Some of these speculators were identified and should have been interrogated. The FBI could have offered leniency in exchange for identification of sources and, in so doing, dismantle criminal networks. Was this what they chose to do? Dennis Lormel, Chief of the Financial Crimes Section at the Criminal Investigations Division of the FBI, made the following comment at the Committee on Financial Services of the U.S. House of Representatives on October 3, 2001.

> To date there are no flags or indicators that the people that were associated with this particular attack, nor are there any indications that people took advantage of this. That is certainly not to say that didn't happen, and there are certainly some rumors out there to that effect, but we are fully exploring that. And as I said, we have a team totally dedicated to that aspect of the investigation.[251]

The "debate" would go no further as the chairman of the committee, the Hon. Michael G. Oxley, declared that "The gentleman's time has expired" and thanked those present for their participation. Kyle Fence then stated:

> In light of the weighty and compelling evidence, Lormel's insistence there were "no flags or indicators" of possible terrorist insider trading, is blatantly wrong or worse, suspect. Most of the information above, including Bloomberg trading charts documenting massive put options spikes, was in the public domain prior to his testimony. Yet, Lormel claimed there was no indication of suspicious trading. Why then were investigations launched by over a dozen nations and 8 or 9

---

251. http://commdocs.house.gov/committees/bank/hba75656.000/hba75656_0.HTM

U.S. government agencies, exchanges and commissions? How does one account for supporting comments of the traders and analysts with years of hands-on experience in the markets?

Lormel's testimony, coming from an official charged with tracking down, and starving terrorists of funding to protect Americans does little to inspire confidence; especially in the wake of the worst intelligence failure in US history. On the contrary, such remarks only raise very uncomfortable suspicions and legitimate concern that the forces behind walls of financial secrecy are so powerful as to thwart or intimidate the highest echelon of those responsible for executing our nation's war on terrorism. Or on drug trafficking. Or on Economic tax evasion and corporate fraud for that matter.

The obvious challenge for authorities is to put these suspicions to rest and follow the money trail to those complicit in the attacks.[252]

The question is, who were the accomplices? Is the FBI's role not to identify them? Thus, in Kevin Ryan's previously quoted article, he states:

In May 2007, a 9/11 Commission document that summarized the FBI investigations into potential 9/11-related informed trading was declassified.[21] This document was redacted to remove the names of two FBI agents from the New York office, and to remove the names of select suspects in the informed trading investigations. The names of other FBI agents and suspects were left in.[253]

---

252. http://commdocs.house.gov/committees/bank/hba75656.000/hba75656_0. HTM

253. Note 21: 9/11 Commission memorandum.

The author then gives names, companies—despite at least possible indirect links to al-Qaeda, they would not be interrogated by the FBI (we recommend to read the full article published by *Foreign Policy Journal*[254]). Consequently, here is his conclusion:

> People knew in advance about the crimes of 9/11, and they profited from that knowledge. Those people are among us today, and our families and communities are at risk of future terrorist attacks and further criminal profiteering if we do not respond to the evidence. It is time for an independent, international investigation into the informed trades and the traders who benefited from the terrorist acts of September 11th.[255]

Who can disagree? But, apart from making sure that nothing and no-one would contradict the government version of the conspiracy, what did the FBI do?

---

254. *Evidence for Informed Trading on the Attacks of September 11*, Kevin Ryan, *Foreign Policy Journal*, November 18, 2010, https://www.foreignpolicyjournal.com/2010/11/18/evidence-for-informed-trading-on-the-attacks-of-september-11/.
255. *Evidence for Informed Trading on the Attacks of September 11*, Kevin Ryan, *Foreign Policy Journal*, November 18, 2010.

Chapter 9/11

The FBI Lies

Although this title could apply to almost all previous chapters, further elements are added. These are at least as disturbing, shocking even, considering the number of innocent victims, and raise new questions about the FBI's role in 9/11 — and its complicity?

Impossible Phone Calls

Phone calls were made by passengers and crew members of the hijacked planes to those on the ground. These calls are among the key stones in understanding September 11. Several authors, including Thierry Meyssan, Michel Chossudovsky and David Griffin, have noticed plot holes in this supposedly compelling evidence.

The latter wrote an entire chapter titled *Phone Calls from the 9/11 Planes: How They Fooled America* in his book *9/11 Ten Years Later*. He states:

> These reported phone calls have been of utmost importance to the official story about 9/11. They provided the main basis for the twofold belief that (1) the planes had been hijacked and that (2) the hijackers were from the Middle East.
>
> There is a multi-faceted argument against the official account of 9/11 (according to which the 9/11 attacks were carried out by Muslim members of al-Qaeda). Part of this argument is that the "phone calls from the planes" were not authentic. The present essay provides various types of evidence that the calls were indeed, faked.[256]

---

256. *9/11 Ten Years Later*, David Ray Griffin, p. 124.

The first argument, confirmed by experts, is that in 2001 NO cell phone worked when aircraft were flying at 30,000 to 40,000 feet. Michel Chossudovsky, for example, wrote:

> According to industry experts, the crucial link in wireless cell phone transmission from an aircraft is altitude. Beyond a certain altitude which is usually reached within a few minutes after takeoff, cell phone calls are no longer possible.
>
> In other words, **given the wireless technology available on September 11, 2001, these cell calls could not have been placed from high altitude.**[257]
>
> The only way passengers could have got through to family and friends using their cell phones, is if the planes were flying below 8000 feet. Yet even at low altitude, below 8000 feet, cell phone communication is of poor quality.
>
> The crucial question: at what altitude were the planes traveling, when the calls were placed?[258]

It is indeed crucial, because the answer could reveal that all these phone calls had been impossible to make, which would uncover some of the FBI's lies during the investigation. Michel Chossudovsky continues his article as follows:

> While the information provided by the Commission is scanty, the Report's timeline does not suggest that the planes were consistently traveling at low altitude. In fact the Report confirms that a fair number of the cell phone calls were placed while the plane was traveling at altitudes above 8,000 feet, which is considered as the cutoff altitude for cell phone transmission.

---

257. In bold in the text.
258. *What Happened on the Planes on September 11, 2001? The 9/11 Cell Phone Calls. The 9/11 Commission "Script" Was Fabricated*, Prof Michel Chossudovsky, Global Research, 10 August 2004.

Indeed, some of the listed phone calls were made while flying at high altitude. On Flight UA93, for example, Tom Burnett was apparently at more than 40,000 feet, but got through to his wife, Deena, three times. When questioned, she stated and confirmed to the FBI that her husband had called her from his cell phone. Since it had been his number that flashed on the screen, there was no doubt.

> But with regard to Deena Burnett, as we have seen, there is no ambiguity, because there can be no reasonable way to deny her statement that her husband had called her from his cell phone, because her caller ID showed its number. And there is no reasonable way to deny, we have also seen, that her caller ID did indeed indicate that she had been called from his cell phone.[259]

David Griffin adds further details:

> Even Deena Burnett, who had been a flight attendant, found this puzzling. After writing in her 2006 book that she "looked at the caller ID and indeed it was Tom's cell phone number," she added: "I didn't understand how he could be calling me on his cell phone from the air."[24][260]

As the FBI did not understand either and knew that it was technically impossible, it transformed the facts in its report for the Moussaoui trial five years later, in 2006:

> Why, in light of the fact that Deena Burnett had clearly told the FBI in 2001 that her husband had used his cell phone to

---

259. *9/11 Ten Years Later*, p. 132.
260. Footnote [24]: "Deena L. Burnett (with Anthony F. Giombetti), *Fighting Back: Living Life Beyond Ourselves* (Longwood, Florida, Advantage Inspirational Books, 2006), 61," quoted in *9/11 Ten Years Later*, p. 132.

call her, did the FBI in 2006 stated that Tom Burnett had used passenger-seat phones?

The answer seems to be that the FBI decided to make all of the reports of phone calls from the 9/11 airliners consistent with the evidence that cell phones available in 2001 would not work, at least reliably, from airliners at high altitudes. [...]

Is it not surprising that so many calls that for several years were considered cell phone calls are now designated onboard phone calls by the FBI? Is it really plausible that all of these calls had been made from onboard phones, in spite of the fact that news stories at the time reported that they had been made on cell phones? Does it not appear that the FBI simply changed their reports to prevent the stories about phone calls from being discredited by the evidence that high-altitude phone calls would have been impossible?

Does such investigative procedure not warrant little confidence? What must we believe when the agency in charge is skewing even the most basic facts according to circumstances, its needs and interests? How can we trust it?

If evidence shows that the phone calls Deena received from her husband were made from his cell phone, would it be that complicated for the FBI to get his phone records from the provider? Either his phone calls are not on the list—proving they were faked, or that the flight path was and they flew at low altitude contrary to data—or they are on the record and it was indeed Tom Burnett who called his wife. Then it would not have been necessary to make up a story five years later about calls made from passenger-seat phones. Nevertheless, both versions are worryingly inconsistent:

– if Tom Burnett (and other victims) really called from his cell phone, the plane could not have been flying above 8,000 feet. Therefore, where was it?

– If he made the calls from the passenger-seat phones, they should be on record. Furthermore, this service is not free of charge, meaning Tom Burnett must have used his credit card; such information is easy to verify.

Why did the FBI not provide corresponding evidence to support its two successive and contradictory versions? Is it conceivable that they did not try to gather this evidence? Many innocent people died, this could not have been some rushed investigation.

Unless Tom Burnett's calls appeared neither on his personal records nor on those of passenger-seat phones. That would mean he himself never called.

The reader can imagine the consequences if this conclusion is the good one, and not only on the role and complicity of the FBI.

More Caller Inconsistencies

Tom Burnett's calls are not alone in questioning the FBI's investigation and government version of conspiracy. This book does not seek to deliver a complete analysis of all phone calls and for this it is recommended to read up further on the studies mentioned previously. However, the best-known case, that of Barbara Olson on Flight AA77, which allegedly crashed into the Pentagon, contained particularly relevant information.

In summary, from the plane, she called her husband at the Department of Justice, Theodore Olson, who was Solicitor General. According to his testimony, she had called twice, which was confirmed to the FBI by two members of his team. Yet, versions varied from one to four calls depending on sources and reports. Even though Mr. Olson is convinced his wife called from her cell phone, an FBI report from 2004 excluded this possibility when it concluded:

All of the calls from Flight 77 were made via the onboard airphone system.[261]

The case bears a resemblance to Burnett's, apart from one significant element. Unfortunately for the FBI's version, it appears that there were no such devices on Flight 77, thereby invalidating the claim. It was confirmed by several statements, such as the one below:

> In 2004, Ian Henshall and Rowland Morgan had come to suspect that the Boeing 757s used by American Airlines did not have onboard telephones. Accordingly, they asked American Airlines whether its "757s [are] fitted with phones that passengers can use." An AA spokesperson replied: "American Airlines 757s do not have onboard phones for passenger use." Then, to check on the possibility that Barbara Olson might have borrowed a phone intended for crew use, they asked: "[A]re there any onboard phones at all on AA 757s, i.e., that could be used either by passengers or cabin crew?" The response was: "AA 757s do not have any onboard phones, either for passenger or crew use. Crew have other means of communication available."[262]

Therefore, Barbara Olson could neither have reached her husband from her phone, as stated by the FBI, nor from the onboard system, as stated by American Airlines—her bank account was also not debited for any such services. In brief, she could not have placed a call. Yet, the DoJ received two. So, who called using her identity and gave almost the only known details on the hijackers of Flight 77, stating that they were armed with knives and cutters?

This question holds at least some relevance to the investigation, but

261. *9/11 Ten Years Later*, p. 154.
262. *9/11 Ten Years Later*, p. 154.

still did not interest the FBI. In 2006, America's leading investigative agency concluded that Barbara Olsen had only made one call and that it had lasted zero second. Testimonies made by Theodore Olson and his staff were thus nullified by the Bureau. Whether the Solicitor General had lied or not, the FBI's conclusion would make "managing" the investigation easier. With calls from both tools being deemed impossible, the most visible contradictions were avoided. David Griffin, for example, states:

> *Conclusion*: On the one hand, a combination of evidence shows that Barbara Olson did not make two successful calls to her husband's office from AA77.[127] On the other hand, it seems impossible to deny that Ted Olson's office received two calls that seemed to be from Barbara Olson. When taking these two points together, we must conclude that the Barbara Olson calls were in some sense faked.[263]

A logical conclusion. It leads us to ask why the FBI would fail to investigate such incoherent evidence that could prove destructive to the government narrative? Perhaps the answer lies within the question.

Even More Caller Inconsistencies

Among the other strange phone calls, two were even more peculiar in that they continued AFTER Flight 93 crashed. Let us start with Jeremy Glick, who told Lyzbeth, his wife, that he loved her and not to hang up. She managed to wait several minutes, before distress took over and she handed the phone to her father, Richard Makely. He heard wind-like noises, screams, followed by silence. He stayed connected until 10:45, but the plane crashed between 10:03 and 10:06, at least forty minutes before the call ended. The plane was

---

263. *9/11 Ten Years Later*, p. 159.

obliterated by the force of impact. As such, the connection length is surprising. Equally baffling is that no noise indicating the crash was heard either.

Tod Beamer's case is similar, except that he preferred calling GTE-Verizon employees—Phyllis Johnson and Lisa Jefferson—instead of his wife who was expecting their third child. Lisa Jefferson stated that she did not have time to press the "Record" button, even though the conversation lasted more than ten minutes and the *Pittsburgh Post-Gazette* reported the opposite on September 19, 2001.[264] If the call was indeed recorded, hiding it from the American people adds on to the long list of mysteries that the FBI did not solve.

Lisa Jefferson confirmed that the call had continued in silence for fifteen minutes AFTER the crash and, like Richard Makely, heard no crashing sound. She stated that communication was not cut, otherwise there would have been a characteristic squealing sound; the line simply went silent. Jefferson's words were confirmed by the fact that the call lasted until 10:49, i.e. more than sixty-five minutes, ending well after the moment of impact. For an in-flight cellphone connection, it seems incredible.

While the silent lines and other elements appear strange, there is something even more mystifying:

> 7. On September 29, 2001, the FBI received detailed records from Verizon's wireless subscriber office in Bedminster, NJ, that Todd Beamer's cell phone made 19 outgoing calls after the alleged 10:03 AM crash time of Flight UA93.[22] This fact, along with the sixth one, indicates either that the man self-identified as Todd Beamer was not on UA93, or Tod Beamer's cell phone was not on the flight, or this flight did not crash.[265]

264. *9/11 Ten Years Later*, p. 152.
265. Point PC-1: The Alleged Calls of Todd Beamer, Flight UA 93. Note 22: FBI Lead Control Number NK 5381, 09/29/2001. (Mr. Beamer's cell phone area was in Northern New Jersey [prefix 908], so the records reflect the Eastern Time zone). http://www.consensus911.org/point-pc-1.

On Intelwire.com, Todd Beamer's telephone call records obtained from the FBI show nineteen calls with a masked recipient. Each was made to Woodbridge, New Jersey, lasted one minute, and took place between 11:07 a.m. to 8:58 p.m.[266]

Could one conceive that the FBI did not attempt to uncover the identities of the recipient and caller using Todd Beamer's phone after his death on Flight 93?

This section on the mysterious phone calls will conclude with David Griffin's words:

> The second way of showing that all of the purported calls were inauthentic begins with a few of these calls—such as the Tom Burnett, the CeeCee Lyles, the Betty Ong, the Todd Beamer, and the Barbara Olson calls—which were rather obviously faked. We then move to the point that, if some of the calls were faked, then all of them must have been inauthentic, because if the official account—according to which the planes were hijacked in a surprise operation—were true, then no one would have been prepared to fake any calls.
>
> In any case, the reported "phones from the planes" were central to the processes through which the perpetrators of the 9/11 attacks convinced Americans that these attacks were planned and carried out by Muslims.[267]

In his conclusion on the chapter 5, Griffin even talks of these calls that fooled the American people as a "state crime against democracy." The responsibility and the role—therefore complicity?—of the FBI is immeasurable.

---

266. Intelfiles.egoplex.com/2001-09-29-FBI-phone-records.pdf.
267. *9/11 Ten Years Later*, p. 169.

United Airlines Flight 93

Briefly put, the government version of the conspiracy for this flight, supported by a Hollywood production, reported that passengers resisted the hijackers and heroically crashed the plane in Pennsylvania. Their sacrifice saved the Capitol building, a symbol of American democracy.

If we listen to witnesses rather than Hollywood, a different story appears: Flight 93 was allegedly shot down by military aircraft. In *The New Pearl Harbour*, David Griffin quotes CBS who reported that two F-16 fighter jets had been tailing the plane. A flight controller confirmed that one F-16 had closely pursued it. At least half a dozen witnesses saw another plane flying at low altitude above the crash site. They

> describe the plane as a small, white jet with rear engines and no discernible markings.[268] The FBI claimed that the plane was a Fairchild Falcon 20 business jet. But, said one woman: "It was white with no marking but it was definitely military.... It had two rear engines, a big fin on the back like a spoiler.... It definitely wasn't one of those executive jets. The FBI came and talked to me and said there was no plane around.... But I saw it and it was there before the crash and it was 40 feet above my head. They did not want my story."[269]

Her testimony was not unique:

> For example, local man Dennis Decker says that immediately after hearing an explosion, "We looked up, we saw a midsized jet flying low and fast. It appeared to make a loop or part of a circle, and then it turned fast and headed out. If you were here to see it, you'd have no doubt. It was a jet plane, and it had to

---

268. *Independent*, August 13, 2002, quoted in *The New Pearl Harbor*, p. 51.
269. *The New Pearl Harbour*, p. 52.

be flying real close when that 757 went down . . . If I was the FBI, I'd find out who was driving that plane." (*Bergen Record*, 9/14/01).[270]

Yes, but the FBI was not interested. And regardless, as Webster Griffin Tarpley points out:

> The authorities failed to provide the identity of the owner of the jet, and also could not justify why it was still flying some 40 minutes after the Federal Aviation Administration had ordered all planes to land at the nearest airport.[271]

Other witnesses talked about one or two loud bangs they heard. Some even mentioned a missile being fired. Ernie Stuhl, mayor of Shanksville, relayed this information from residents near the crash site, one of them a Vietnam veteran.[272] This book does not seek to analyze what really happened. However, why did the FBI refuse to consider these testimonies and deny the presence of a (military) plane? Agents even attempted to influence witnesses by telling them that they did not see what they had seen. Does this behavior add to its lies?

---

270. *The Terror Timeline*, p. 494.
271. *9/11 Synthetic Terror Made in USA*, p. 268.
272. *The Terror Timeline*, p. 447.

Flight 93 allegedly disappeared into this hole, from which nothing stood out. How could a Boeing 757 have sunk into the ground without so much as a tail or a wing marking its presence? On September 14, 2001, officials denied that Flight 93 was shot down. However, faced with evidence that undermined the government version, they postulated that hijackers had a bomb on board and blew up the plane. After an on-site investigation, the FBI concluded that no explosives were involved.[273]

Even for a supporter of the government version of the conspiracy, it would be hard to suggest that a Boeing could have been swallowed up by the Earth without a trace. Nothing protruded from the ground, but pieces of wreckage were found some miles from the crash scene. The following examples are noteworthy:
    – at Indian Lake, at about 3 miles;
    – at New Baltimore, some 8 miles away, where they were more numerous;
    – more debris were found 6 miles away, together with human remains;
    – a half-ton piece of turbine was discovered 2,000 yards from the main crash site.[274]
Despite scattered and distant debris fields, more than 8 miles away, the FBI stuck to the government narrative. The plane was allegedly obliterated due to the force of impact and not shot down as evidence would rather suggest. As the FBI version goes, a 500 kg engine "landed" 2,000 yards away, pieces of fuselage "flew" up to 8 miles, despite no bomb being present. Is this credible?

273. *The Terror Timeline*, p. 494.
274. *The Terror Timeline*, p. 492.

Also, civilians were not the only witnesses who contradicted the government. *The Terror Timeline* team relates a testimony from September 11 on p. 464:

> 2:00 p.m.: Fighter Pilot Told Flight 93 Was Shot Down
> F-15 fighter pilot Major Daniel Nash returns to base around this time, after chasing Flight 175 and patrolling the skies over New York City. He says that when he gets out of the plane, "he [is] told that a military F-16 had shot down a fourth airliner in Pennsylvania..." (*Cape Code Times*, 8/21/02; *Aviation Week and Space Technology*, 6/3/02).

The FBI cannot admit that Flight 93 was shot down. Although it would not inherently question the events as recited by officials, it would open a Pandora's Box with a plethora of questions: Why would they shoot it down, who gave the order, under whose authority, was it the only option, especially if passengers were allegedly fighting the hijackers, etc.?

American Airlines Flight 77

The lies spread by the FBI about this plane are among the most blatant of the whole 9/11 Operation. In Chapter 9/7, it was shown that the FBI seized all tapes likely to show what had happened in Washington, losing some in the process—accidentally? Is it normal for an intelligence agency to "misplace" critical evidence?

What struck more attentive observers is the fact that a plane had literally disappeared into a hole on the ground floor of the Pentagon. It was a mere 6 meters wide and did not damage the rest of the façade nor the front lawn. A Boeing 757 of the 200 series is a sizable aircraft: 47.32 meters long, with a wingspan of 38 meters (41.10 meters including winglets),12 meters high to the tip of its tail with landing gear retracted and weighing in at 58 tons empty.

Experts and self-proclaimed debunkers explain that it is possible physically. The most credible base their arguments on an impact width of about 20 meters. But a hole of this size appeared only after the facade collapsed around 10:10, i.e. more than half an hour after the plane had officially crashed into the Pentagon. Some "experts," mainly anonymous, even state that the colossal impact folded the wings and engines along the cabin, explaining by nothing other that the lower windows had been damaged. One would be hard-pressed to find a physical explanation for how the plane's wings could fold, engines and all. Considering the speed at which the plane hit the building, this would have taken place during a fraction of a second. How could it be possible with all that weight?

These explanations are ridiculous and would be laughable, had there not been 184 innocent victims. 125 of them were from the Pentagon with most being Army and Navy; there were no US Air Force victims. Let us bring up former DIA Office of Naval Intelligence (ONI) employee, E.P. Heidner[275], and his stunning study. According to him, the real reason for the Pentagon attack was related to ONI's office, of which 39 of 40 members were killed. They were investigating a $240 billion fraud case and Heidner, among others, alleges that covering up these operations had been the main purpose of 9/11.

Within the realm of this hypothesis, the destruction of the three WTC was also necessary to halt investigations, among which was a possible FBI inquiry into Barrick Gold, a world reference in gold mining, in which Adnan Kashoggi was a key figure.

Maybe the torture and death of his nephew, Jamal, at the Saudi consulate at Ankara, did not only concern his opposition to bin Salman's regime. Was he worth such a risk? Or was he tortured to reveal information on gold stores plundered by the Japanese in Asia during the first half of the 20th Century? Indeed, it appears these

---

275. *Collateral Damage: U.S. Covert Operations and the Terrorist Attacks on September 11, 2001*, EP Heidner, 28 June, 2008, https://wikispooks.com/w/images/d/db/Collateral_Damage_-_part_1.pdf.

reserves were never returned to Japan nor the countries from which they had been stolen (China, Korea, etc.). Did private entities in the United States take all or some of this gold? Were Barrick Gold and Kashoggi being used as part of an elaborate laundering operation through their facilities in Switzerland?[276]

Back to the FBI.

Faced with a wall of doubt around the little damage caused by the 757, the government narrative received the support of The American Society of Civil Engineers in 2003, which drew up *The Pentagon Building Performance Report*. One of the most detailed counter-analyses we read was done by Sami Yli-Karjanmaa in September 2004, with an update in April 2007. Here follows an extract:

> The key conclusion reached is that **the *Report* fails in its attempt to show that the structural damage caused to the Pentagon on Sept. 11, 2001 was caused by a crash by a Boeing 757 aircraft.**[277] The main purpose of the *Report* seems therefore to be to back the official, untruthful story about the events of 9/11. However, part of the inconsistencies are so glaring that an intention of sabotaging the said main purpose cannot be excluded.
>
> The key conclusion is based on nine observations which can be divided into two categories based on whether they concern events prior to or during the crash of the aircraft. As regards the first group, the overall conclusion is that the approach of the aircraft and its being damaged cannot have taken place in the manner put forward in the *Report*. This conclusion is supported by the following observations:

---

276. *Collateral Damage: U.S. Covert Operations and the Terrorist Attacks on September 11, 2001*, EP Heidner, 28 June, 2008, https://wikispooks.com/w/images/d/db/Collateral_Damage_-_part_1.pdf.
277. Characters in bold in the original document.

– the aircraft's reported 42° approach angle is not possible for a B-757;

– the aircraft's right wing's hitting a generator cannot account for the narrowness and discontinuity of the damage to the facade as proposed by the *Report*;

– the intact cable spools in the trajectory of the aircraft are incompatible with the information on the impact contained in the *Report*; and,

– there is no evidence to support the claim of the left engine having hit a vent structure; such a hit would also not explain the narrowness of the damage to the facade.

Sami Yli-Karjanmaa then makes a second group of observations:

[...] the overall conclusion is that the *Report*'s description of the impact of the plane and of the damage caused manifestly contradicts photographic evidence from the scene. The description includes impossible, contradictory and unexplained phenomena:

– the allegation of the aircraft's fuselage sliding into the first floor has no physical credibility;

– the facade damage on the right side of the opening in the outer wall does not correspond to the shape, size and reported position of the alleged B-757;

– the facade damage on the left side of the opening are not suggestive of the proposed impact of a B-757;

– the tail of the aircraft left no visible marks on the facade while the *Report* in no way explains this; and,

– the *Report* fails to provide any kind of explanation for the hole in the wall of Ring C.

The uncertainties related to the alleged point of impact as well as the approach angle, vertical position and inclination of the aircraft do not weaken the conclusion presented herein that **the Pentagon could not have been hit by a Boeing 757** in the manner described in the *Report*. This is because changing one of these factors to allow the better explanation of a particular damage (or the lack of it) renders the other damage even less comprehensible.[278]

Consequently, the author reaches this conclusion:

The Pentagon Building Performance Report by the American Society of Civil Engineers fails in its attempt to show that the structural damage caused to the Pentagon on Sept. 11, 2001 was caused by a crash by a Boeing 757 aircraft. Belief in the official B-757 story implies belief in physically impossible and inexplicable phenomena. […]
The most natural explanation for the numerous errors in the Report is that it is a part of the disinformation campaign by the US authorities — the purpose of which is to prevent the truth regarding 9/11 from being revealed and thus to protect the perpetrators of those atrocities.

If Sami Yli-Karjanmaa is right, would it not undeniably suggest complicity? How did the FBI react? All the more as Pilots for 9/11 Truth[279] published an article during the same period, on March 26, 2007. They petitioned the National Transportation and Safety Board (NTSB) via the Freedom of Information Act to obtain their 2002 report, *Flight Path Study-American Airlines Flight 77*. The report

---

278. *The ASCE's Pentagon Building Performance Report, Arrogant Deception- Or an Attempt to Expose a Cover-up?*, Sami Yli-Karjanmaa, April 13, 2007,http://www.kolumbus.fi/sy-k/pentagon/asce_en.htm..
279. "Pilots for 9/11 Truth is an organization of aviation professionals and pilots throughout the globe who have gathered together for one purpose. We are committed to seeking the truth surrounding the events of the 11th of September 2001. Our main focus concentrates on the four flights, maneuvers performed and the reported pilots. […]." www.pilotsfor911truth.org.

consisted of a Comma Separated Value (CSV) file and Flight Path Animation, allegedly derived from Flight 77's Flight Data Recorder (FDR). Here is the conclusion:

> The data provided by the NTSB contradict the 9/11 Commission Report in several significant ways:
> 1. The NTSB Flight Path Animation approach path and altitude does not support official events.
> 2. All Altitude data shows the aircraft at least 300 feet too high to have struck the light poles.
> 3. The rate of descent data is in direct conflict with the aircraft being able to impact the light poles and be captured in the Dept of Defense "5 Frames" video of an object traveling nearly parallel with the Pentagon lawn.
> 4. The record of data stops at least one second prior to official impact time.
> 5. If data trends are continued, the aircraft altitude would have been at least 100 feet too high to have hit the Pentagon.
> In August, 2006, members of Pilots for 9/11 Truth received these documents from the NTSB and began a close analysis of the data they contain. After expert review and cross check, Pilots for 9/11 Truth has concluded that the information in these NTSB documents does not support, and in some instances factually contradicts, the official government position that American Airlines Flight 77 struck the Pentagon on the morning of September 11, 2001.[280]

Naturally, the FBI seems not to have looked at these disturbing analyses that refute the presence of Flight 77 at the Pentagon. Probably because everybody knows that Muslim fanatics succeeded all alone in executing an unprecedented operation against the most formidable military and intelligence organization in history.

---

280. *Official Account of 9/11 Flight Contradicted by Government's Own Data*, www. pilotsfor911truth.org.

Missing Wreckage

Another puzzling problem with the government version story of Flight 77 is the apparent "disappearance" of the wreckage, whereas a Boeing 757-200 weighs 58 tons empty, to which must be added passengers, luggage, fuel, etc. This is a key point in my suggestion that Thierry Meyssan write *9/11 The Big Lie* and *Pentagate*. Far-fetched comments were thrown around in the French media and others explaining that the plane "gasified." Aluminum can transform into gas, but it would require a temperature of at least 5,400° F; it is impossible for a jet fuel blaze to reach even half that intensity.

Nevertheless, they noticed that material was missing. In support of the doubt around Flight 77's presence, in *9/11 The Big Lie* Thierry Meyssan reported on a Pentagon press conference led by Victoria Clarke, Deputy Secretary of Defense, on September 12. Arlington County fire chief, Ed Plaugher, said that

> his men were employed in fighting the fire's spread within the Pentagon, but had been kept away from the immediate crash site. Only the FEMA's special Urban Search and Rescue teams came into contact with the plane.
>
> A surreal dialogue then took place during this press conference:
>
> Reporter: "Is there anything left of the aircraft at all?"
>
> Plaugher: "First all, the question about the aircraft, there are some small pieces of aircraft visible from the interior during this fire-fighting operation I'm talking about, but not large sections. In other words, there's no fuselage sections and that sort of thing."
>
> [...]
>
> Reporter: "Chief, there are small pieces of the plane virtually all over, out over the highway, tiny pieces. Would you say the plane exploded, virtually exploded on impact due to the fuel or...?"
>
> Plaugher: "You know, I'd rather not comment on that. We have

a lot of eyewitnesses that can give you better information about what actually happened with the aircraft as it approached. So we don't know. I don't know."

[...]

Reporter: "Where is the jet fuel? Just ...?"

Plaugher: "We have what we believe is a puddle right there that the... what we believe is to be the nose of the aircraft" (sic).

So, although officials, members of Congress and military personnel all claimed to have seen the aircraft fall, no one saw the smallest piece of the plane, not even from the landing gear: there were only unidentifiable metal fragments.[281]

In *Pentagate,* we read that on September 15, at another press conference, it was confirmed that no decisive fragments of the plane had been uncovered and that only "small pieces" were visible as declared by the DoD representative. Officially, only two black boxes and a beacon were uncovered. Even the debris on the picture taken by Mark Faram does not fit the aircraft (see on next page). Thus, the situation can be described as follows:

In the first days following the attack, the authorities therefore mentioned only the existence of small debris, unidentifiable metallic fragments, which could have been from something quite different.

None of the firemen, architects or DoD officials saw any piece of the fuselage on the site of the attack-with the exception of the Secretary of Defense, Donald Rumsfeld.[282]

---

281. *9/11 The Big Lie*, pp. 23-24.
282. *Pentagate*, p. 19.

U.S. Navy Photo by Journalist 1st Class Mark D. Faram

Witnesses later surfaced, explaining that they saw large pieces of the plane, even fuselage, directly contradicting the Pentagon version. They also claimed that pictures were taken. As far as we know none were ever made public. Why?

> And how is it that the Pentagon, which only found, officially, a beacon and two black boxes, was unaware of all this debris from the Boeing on its own lawn?[283]

---

283. *Pentagate*, p. 23.

Even on the FBI official website[284], only the three following pictures of debris were published:

The red serial number and C could indicate American Airlines ownership, despite their small size compared to that of a Boeing 757-200. Logically, Flight 77 indeed crashed into the Pentagon. Yet—and this is without acknowledging that the FBI has proven itself entirely capable of forging evidence in Operation 9/11—what happened to the rest of the plane? It is easy to answer that the FBI only took or showed three pictures, but that there were other fragments. This contradicts all the DoD statements, included those of the September 15 conference. In four days, the military had more than enough time to identify all the pieces found.

Therefore, in *9/11 Ten Years Later*, starting at page 212, David Griffin lists several testimonies made by Pentagon employees stating that they did not see any plane fragments nor damage likely to have been caused by a Boeing 757. Although, seven months later:

> The FBI's statement is troubling: its agents are said to have recovered a large part of the debris, allowing an almost complete restoration of the Boeing. The latter was confirmed by Chris Murray, FBI spokesman in Washington [...]. Thus, the plane was not smashed into small fragments as stated by the

---

284. FBI Records: The Vault – 9/11 Attacks and Investigation Images, https://vault.fbi.gov/9-11-attacks-investigation-and-related-materials/9-11-images.

Pentagon in September 2001. [...] Far from it, in April 2002, the plane could nearly be reconstituted by the FBI.[285]

"The white arrow represents the trajectory of the aircraft, and its point, the place where "its nose came out."

in *Pentagate* (XV)

As there was no fuselage outside (confirmed by the parking lot camera, nothing protruded from the building after the explosion), how should we believe that a 47.32m long, 38 m wide Boeing 757 crashed into the building? Since they could not vaporize or be gasified, where are the nearly 60 tons of parts?

As soon as the FBI declared that it was able reconstitute the plane almost entirely, the question is who lied: the Bureau, or the DoD and the first witnesses, among them military, who only saw fragments

---

285. *Pentagate*, p. 20.

and no trace of an airliner inside the building, as confirmed by pictures taken on that day? And even if this quasi-Boeing stored in an FBI warehouse was shown, it would have been easy to fake and thus it would be of little significance.

Nevertheless, note that the FBI managed to collect fragments that nobody had seen and where there were none, and nearly rebuild an entire plane.

No Terrorists in the Cockpit

On November 27, 2009, Pilots For 9/11 Truth published an article titled *9/11: Pentagon Aircraft Hijack Impossible-Flight Deck Door Closed for Entire Flight*:

> Newly decoded data provided by an independent researcher and computer programmer from Australia exposes alarming evidence that the reported hijacking aboard American Airlines Flight 77 was impossible to have existed.[286]

This piece of evidence analyzed a flight parameter called "Flight Deck Door" to determine whether the deck door had been opened during flight. The results for Flight 77 were communicated by the National Transportation Safety Board (NTSB), an official agency. Here is how the article continues:

> On the morning of September 11, 2001, American Airlines Flight 77 departed Dulles International Airport bound for Los Angeles at 8:20 am Eastern Time. According to reports and data, a hijacking took place between 08:50:54 and 08:54:11 in which the hijackers allegedly crashed the aircraft into the Pentagon at 09:37:45. Reported by CNN, according to Ted Olson, wife Barbara Olson had called him from the reported

---

286. http://pilotsfor911truth.org/forum/index.php?showtopic=18405

flight stating, "...all passengers and flight personnel, including the pilots, were herded to the back of the plane by armed hijackers..." However, according to Flight Data provided by the NTSB, the Flight Deck Door was never opened in flight. How were the hijackers able to gain access to the cockpit, remove the pilots, and navigate the aircraft to the Pentagon if the Flight Deck Door remained closed?

A pertinent question that the FBI should have looked at. As a matter of fact, it still would not be too late to verify the analysis of the Australian researcher and Pilots For 9/11 Truth, especially since such a small parameter debunks the government's statements concerning Flight 77. To a broader extent, it would dismantle their 9/11 narrative. It would also be worth checking the data for the other aircraft.

No Squawks

A transponder, or transmitter-responder device, allows airlines to send signals based on four-digit codes, otherwise known as "squawks." Their meanings vary from country to country, but three of these codes are universal in order to quickly warn air traffic controllers:
- 7500: Aircraft hijacking;
- 7600: Radio failure;
- 7700: Emergency.

All pilots know these codes, yet not a single one of the four hijacked planes transmitted squawk 7500. Given the high level of experience of the pilots, it was said that the element of surprise had deprived them of the few seconds needed to squawk.

However, it is not true, at least in Flight 93's case, as the FBI broadcast a soundtrack during the Moussaoui trial where the pilots shouted "Mayday! Mayday! Mayday!" as terrorists entered the cockpit, and then, thirty seconds later, "Mayday! Get out of here! Get out of here!"[287]

It proves that they were still alive, and, simultaneously, that they had enough time to squawk 7500 before hijackers breached the flight deck. Their failure to do so remains a mystery.

In Flight 77's case, there was no squawk and the Flight Deck Door parameter showed that the door was not opened. Despite this, Theodore Olson relayed his wife's statement that the pilots and passengers had been grouped at the back of the plane by the terrorists. Does this make the government version of the hijacking credible? Could the FBI, although in charge of the investigation, not have noticed the ocean of inconsistencies and contradictions in this version of the conspiracy?

Far-Away Signals After Impact

In addition to the transponder, which can be disconnected by pilots and make the plane disappear from certain types of radar, there is an Aircraft Communication Addressing and Reporting System, or ACARS, allowing for encrypted communication with ground stations. ACARS messages are used in air traffic, aeronautical operational or administrative control. The Wikipedia extract below provides more information:

> Automated ping messages are used to test an aircraft's connection with the communication station. In the event that the aircraft ACARS unit has been silent for longer than a preset time interval, the ground station can ping the aircraft (directly or via satellite). A ping response indicates a healthy ACARS communication.[288]

---

287. *9/11 Ten Years Later*, p. 29.
288. en.wikipedia.org/wiki/ACARS

It is important to note that the system is designed to route messages through the nearest ground station, much like the way cellphones use relay antennas. Therefore, a flight leaving from Chicago to Houston will exchange ACARS messages with different stations along its flight path and not only the two cities.

Flight 175's ACARS messages were acquired thanks to the Freedom of Information Act (FOIA). PilotsFor911Truth.org analyzed the data:

> This message was sent on Sept 11, at 1259Z (8:59AM Eastern) to United Flight 175, tail number N612UA, routed through the MDT remote ground station (Harrisburg International Airport, also known as Middleton).[289]

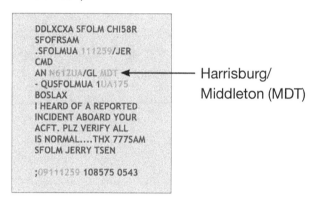

Harrisburg/
Middleton (MDT)

Thus, at 8:59, Flight 175, which would crash into the South Tower in four minutes, was in Pennsylvania.155 miles separate Harrisburg from New York, and a Boeing 767 could not cover it so quickly. At 9:03, the time of impact, two more ACARS messages were sent to the plane and again routed through Harrisburg, meaning it was in the vicinity. Were it not the case, they would have been sent through New York on approach to the WTC. How could the plane have been in two different locations at the same time?

---

289. *Acars Confirmed – 9/11 Aircraft Airborne Long After Crash – United 175 in the Vicinity of Harrisburg and Pittsburgh, PA*, PilotsFor911Truth.org.

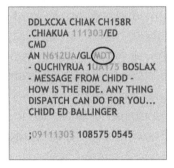

```
DDLXCXA CHIAK CH158R
.CHIAKUA 111303/ED
CMD
AN N612UA/GL MDT
- QUCHIYRUA 1UA175 BOSLAX
- MESSAGE FROM CHIDD -
HOW IS THE RIDE. ANY THING
DISPATCH CAN DO FOR YOU...
CHIDD ED BALLINGER

;09111303 108575 0545
```

```
DDLXCXA CHIYR CH158R
.CHIYRUA 111303/AD
CMD
AN N612UA/GL MDT
- QUCHIYRUA 1UA175 BOSLAX
- MESSAGE FROM CHIDD -
NY APROACH LOOKIN FOR YA
ON 127.4
CHIDD AD ROGERS

;09111303 108575 0546
```

Even more surprisingly, twenty minutes later, at 9:23, another ACARS message was sent to the Boeing, by then burning within the South Tower. It routed through Pittsburgh, which is more than 315 miles west of New York and in the complete opposite direction beyond Harrisburg. It is technically **impossible** that a message routed to a plane in New York be delivered through Pittsburg; the distance is far too great and the closest ground station always delivers the message, which should have been New York:

```
DDLXCXA CHIAK CH158R
.CHIAKUA DA 111323/ED
CMD
AN N612UA/GL PIT
- QUCHIYRUA 1UA175 BOSLAX
- MESSAGE FROM CHIDD -
/BEWARE ANY COCKPIT
INTROUSION: TWO AIRCAFT
IN NY . HIT TRADE C
NTER BUILDS...
CHIDD ED BALLINGER

;09111323 108575 0574
```

For confirmation, Pilots For 911 Truth questioned an expert from Arinc, an ACARS network communication protocol provider. She preferred to remain anonymous, and her answer makes it easy to understand why:

When told about the ACARS message being routed through PIT after the airplane had already allegedly crashed into the South Tower, this is what she had to say: "There is no way that this message would be routed through Pittsburgh if the airplane crashed in New York City."

The only conclusion that can be drawn is that Flight 175 was not the plane that crashed into the South Tower. The FBI cannot ignore these facts.

It is not the only flight that completely contradicts the FBI-validated government version of the conspiracy. ACARS messages were also analyzed for Flight 93, that allegedly crashed at Shanksville, Pennsylvania. They show that the plane was about 540 miles from the crash site when it allegedly happened. As shocking as this information is, the reader may think that the FBI was simply not aware of it. Pilots For 911 Truth provides an answer:

> On January 28, 2002, Mr. Winter[290] gave an interview to the FBI at United Headquarters near Chicago, IL(1). During this interview, Mr. Winter reviewed a list of ACARS messages explaining the contents and which messages were received or rejected. The messages provided below are the most significant and fatal to what we have been told by the 9/11 Commission. Two messages were routed through the Fort Wayne, Indiana remote ground stations (FWA), followed by two more messages which were routed through Champaign, IL (CMI). [...]
> There are 10 remote ground stations closer to the flight path than FWA, even more if including CMI ground station in Champaign, IL which is nearly 500 miles from the Shanksville crater. However, according to Mr. Winter, United 93 received

---

290. At that time, Michael J. Winter is Manager of Flight Dispatch for United Air-lines.

messages from CMI remote ground station in Champaign, IL more than 7 minutes after the alleged crash.[291]

The article continues with a copy of Michael Winter's ACARS analysis:

Continuation of FD-302 of   Michael J. Winter   , On 01-28-2002   . Page   3

Message #13 was sent to the aircraft from UAL San Francisco, CA line maintenance to the ACARS screen and also activated the audible signal. The RGS for the message was near Toledo, OH as designated "TOL" in the line "AN N591UA/GL TOL....".

Messages #14 and #15 were sent to the aircraft from CHIDD using the RGS near Toledo, OH. The messages were sent to the ACARS printer.

Messages #16 and #17 were sent to the aircraft from CHIDD using the RGS near Ft. Wayne, IN FWA as designated in the line "AN N591UA/GL FWA...". The messages were sent to the ACARS printer.

Messages #18 and #19 were sent to the aircraft from CHIDD using the RGS near Champaign, IL CMI as designated in the line "AN N591UA/GL CMI....". Both messages were sent to the printer and Message #19 also activated an audible signal in the aircraft.

Messages #20 to #24 were sent to the aircraft from CHIDD. However, all of the messages were rejected indicating the aircraft did not receive them.

Also present during part of this interview was David Knerr, Manager Flight Dispatch Automation, UAL WHQ.

[PDF page 3]

As one can see, messages N° 18 and 19 were delivered through Champaign, 540 miles from Shanksville—19 activated a beeping tone on the plane. Messages 20 to 24 were rejected, which means the plane did not receive them. In fact, the system was designed so that the sender knew whether his message had been delivered, with failure automatically triggering a warning. The article by Pilots For 911 Truth continues as follows:

---

291. *It Is Conclusive – 9/11 Aircraft Airborne Well After Crash –United 93 in the Vicinity of Fort Wayne, Indiana And Champaign, Illinois at Time of Shanksville Alleged Crash*, PilotsFor911Truth.org.

[...] it can be determined that TOL [Toledo] and FWA are not the best stations for routing messages, however routing through CMI is completely absurd if the aircraft in fact crashed in Shanksville. Furthermore, according to the NTSB animation reconstruction, the aircraft allegedly crashed in Shanksville at 10:03 a.m.(4). How can the aircraft possibly receive a message activating an audible signal in the airplane at 1410 (10:10 a.m. Eastern)? It can't if it crashed in Shanksville, it can if it were in the vicinity of CMI. Finally, there is no possible way that an aircraft can receive a message from a remote ground station which is 500+ miles away. The range for remote ground stations is 200 miles, and that is only guaranteed above 29,000 feet(5).

Pilots For 911 Truth then cross-referenced other data with that of Flight 93:

04/28/09 (PilotsFor911Truth.org) – Recently it has been brought to our attention that Air Traffic Control (ATC) transcripts reveal United 93 as being airborne after its alleged crash. Similar scenarios have been offered with regard to American 77 and American 11 showing an aircraft target continuing past its alleged crash point in the case of American 11, or past the turn-around point in the case of American 77. However, both these issues can be easily explained by "Coast Mode" radar tracking. This is not the case with United 93.[292]

This is followed by technical explanations, extracts from transcripts of exchanges by air traffic control provided by the FAA— we recommend reading the full article, which ends with:

It is impossible for ATC to have observed United 93 transponder

---

292. *United 93 Still Airborne After Alleged Crash – According To ATC/Radar*, http://pilotsfor911truth.org/united-93-still-airborne.html.

and altitude after the reported impact time and southeast of the crash site, if United 93 did in fact crash in Shanksville as the 9/11 Commission would have you believe.

By assembling these facts along with those that we did not discuss here, Pilots For 911 Truth unsurprisingly concludes:

It is conclusive, the 9/11 Aircraft were airborne long after their alleged crashes.[293]

Still More ACARS Issues

Adding to the strangeness is a list of ACARS messages sent to Flight 175 by Ed Ballinger—United Airlines flight dispatcher in charge of all United's East to West coast flights on the morning of 9/11. An official document published in 2009, apparently via the FOIA, shows a table of messages to and from United Aircraft, including 175 and 93, between 13:00 and 14:08 UTC.[294]

ACARS Messages From Dispatch; Messages from Aircraft to Ed Ballinger and Chad McCurdy; and Messages to Flights 93*
Sorted by time from 1300-1408Z

Time	MSG FROM	A/C	MSG TO	Route	Full text message
1350	John Dester	N854UA	1481	MIA-ORD	NATIONAL EMERGENCY
1350	Jim Hansen	N372UA	2410	ONT-SFO	OK SFO
1350	David Hora	N872UA	717	ORD-LAS	BASED ON UR LOCATION GO TO OMA
1350	John Bashman	N815UA	1870	DFW-DFW	DID YOU GET MSG TO RETURN TO DFW...
1350	Ed Ballinger	N591UA	93	EWR-SFO	LAND ASP AT NEAREST --NEAREST AIRPORT ASP ASP ON GROND ANYWERE.
2302					
1304					
1351	Roger Canterbury	M669UA	951	BRU-IAD	DIVERT/RETURN TO BRL CONFIRMED...RWC
1351	Chuck Baughman	N349UA	467	BOL-DEN	NATIONWIDE GRND STOP. PLS LAND
1351	Larry Kelly	N660UA	975	LHR-SFO	REF WORLD TRADE CNTR CRASH. TWO A/C WERE HIJACKED THIS MORNING AND THEY BOTH CRASHED INTO THE WORLD TRADE CNTR IN NEW YORK ONE AA & ONE UA BOTH FLTS WERE FROM BOS. ALL ACFT ARE ADVZD TO LIMIT COCKPIT ACCESS. A/C SECURITY ON HIGH ALERT NATION-WIDE
1351	Larry Kelly	N791UA	901	FRA-SFO	REF WORLD TRADE CNTR CRASH. TWO A/C WERE HIJACKED THIS MORNING AND THEY BOTH CRASHED INTO THE WORLD TRADE CNTR IN NEW YORK ONE AA & ONE UA BOTH FLTS WERE FROM BOS. ALL ACFT ARE ADVZD TO LIMIT COCKPIT ACCESS. A/C SECURITY ON HIGH ALERT NATION-WIDE
1351	Larry Kelly	N206UA	988	LHR-SFO	REF WORLD TRADE CNTR CRASH. TWO A/C WERE HIJACKED THIS MORNING AND THEY BOTH CRASHED INTO THE WORLD TRADE CNTR IN NEW YORK ONE AA & ONE UA BOTH FLTS WERE FROM BOS. ALL ACFT ARE ADVZD TO LIMIT COCKPIT ACCESS. A/C SECURITY ON HIGH ALERT NATION-WIDE
1351	Larry Kelly	N657UA	974	SFO-LHR	REF WORLD TRADE CNTR CRASH. TWO A/C WERE HIJACKED THIS MORNING AND THEY BOTH CRASHED INTO THE WORLD TRADE CNTR IN NEW YORK ONE AA & ONE UA BOTH FLTS WERE FROM BOS. ALL ACFT ARE ADVZD TO LIMIT COCKPIT ACCESS. A/C SECURITY ON HIGH ALERT NATION-WIDE
1351	Larry Kelly	N194UA	945	FRA-ORD	REF WORLD TRADE CNTR CRASH. TWO A/C WERE HIJACKED THIS MORNING AND THEY BOTH CRASHED INTO THE WORLD TRADE CNTR IN NEW YORK ONE AA & ONE UA BOTH FLTS WERE FROM BOS. ALL ACFT ARE ADVZD TO LIMIT COCKPIT ACCESS. A/C SECURITY ON HIGH ALERT NATION-WIDE
1351	Larry Kelly	N584UA	945	MUC-IAD	REF WORLD TRADE CNTR CRASH. TWO A/C WERE HIJACKED THIS MORNING AND THEY BOTH CRASHED INTO THE WORLD TRADE CNTR IN NEW YORK ONE AA & ONE UA BOTH FLTS WERE FROM BOS. ALL ACFT ARE ADVZD TO LIMIT COCKPIT ACCESS. A/C SECURITY ON HIGH ALERT NATION-WIDE

Notes: Messages from aircraft are shaded.
EB = Ed Ballinger
CM = Chad McCurdy

* Because the times were not broken down into seconds, the messages from the aircraft were inserted at the beginning of each minute in this chart.

WARNING
THIS DOCUMENT CONTAINS
SENSITIVE SECURITY
INFORMATION

47

UASSI100036075

---

293. In bold in the original text.
294. T7 B18 United AL 9-11 ACARS Fdr- Entire Contents- ACARS Messages 569.pdf.

What draws our attention first is that all messages emitted by the planes have been made unreadable. What needs to be hidden remains a mystery. Surprisingly, the timeline was also cut off at 14:08 UTC / 10:08 EDT (EDT = East Coast time). Yet, 911acars, a specialized blog, points out:

> As widely known to many ACARS researchers, seven uplink messages were sent out from UAL dispatchers to United 93 between 14:10 UTC and 14:20 UTC (Messages #18 – 25 in Winter's list) and therefore they are not reported in this document. While there is still a fierce debate as to whether and which of such messages were received by the aircraft, it is an ascertained and unquestionable fact that they were sent. Therefore, we would expect that the timeline would end at least at 14:30 UTC, if not later, so that all messages related to United 93 would be included in the chart. Remarkably, messages to and from other United aircraft of secondary importance were included in this table, but for some unspecified reason the last seven messages to United 93, one of the four aircraft involved in 9/11, were not. Again, we won't speculate here about the reasons of such decision. However, the fact that the timeline ends at an unexpected time such as 14:08 UTC, along with the exclusion of messages to United 93 which are of vital importance for the ACARS research on 9/11, is something that we wouldn't hesitate to define as suspicious.[295]

No further comment is needed: all useful information was redacted from the official document. Why? Normally, such short exchanges contain no secrets. Would the pilots' words somehow discredit the government version of the conspiracy?

---

295. *Ed Ballinger and the uplink sent to United 175 at 9:51 EDT*, http://911acars. blogspot.com/2012/03/ed-ballinger-and-uplink-sent-to-united.html, March, 7, 2012.

We studied this document in detail. Although the messages sent by the aircraft were made unreadable—the document says "Messages from aircraft are shaded"—we were able to construct a complete list of the planes that sent them. Not surprisingly, there are no anomalies as this document was drawn up with selected data (but there are mistakes on the tail numbers).

The only information available concerns:

    1. "Acars Messages From Dispatch,"

    2. "Messages from Aircraft to Ed Ballinger and Chad McCurdy,"

    3. "Messages to Flights 93."

Why does Flight 175 not show up? Nevertheless, two messages were sent to it at 13:03 (see p. 1 of the document), at the exact minute when it officially crashed into the South Tower:

    – Ed Ballinger: "HOW IS THE RIDE. ANY THING DISPATCH CAN DO FOR YOU."

    – AD Rogers: "NY APPROACH LOOKING FOR YA ON 127.4".

Consequently, if the plane that was in Pennsylvania instead of New York (according to ACARS) replied to AD Rogers, we cannot see it as, unfortunately, any messages he received were removed. Was it done intentionally? And why not give all four planes' ACARS messages in the first place?

Flight 175 has its own set of disturbing data that can be summarized as follows: the plane officially crashed into the South Tower at 9:03 EDT. However, Ed Ballinger made contact twice after the disaster: at 9:23 and 9:51, in which he asked the pilots to "'Land ASAP at the nearest airport." Yet, the plane had crashed 48 minutes earlier, and Ballinger would later testify that he had received news of the aircraft's demise at 9:24. But still he sent the second message. Why ask a plane to land at the nearest airport knowing that it had flown into a building almost 50 minutes earlier? As the 911acars blog states:

The first obvious question raised by this new evidence is 'why' should Ballinger send such an order ("Land asap at the nearest airport") to the cockpit of United 175 at 9:51 EDT if he did not know from some source that the aircraft was actually still airborne.

The logic checks out. However, on p. 48 of *T7 B18 United AL 9-11 ACARS Fdr–Entire Contents–ACARS Messages 569* we learn that Ed Ballinger sent this message to a dozen or so planes, and twice to Flight 93. Considering the situation, he could have mistakenly sent it to Flight 175.

On the other hand, at 10:40 he informed Flight 93 that flights 93 and 175 were missing. But a minute later, he made contact again to say that they had been found. Did he receive any information during that minute?

Naturally, none of these questions were asked by the Commission nor the FBI. But these authorities were not the only parties involved in the cover-up, as 911acars concluded:

> Why is this log missing in the UAL record of Ballinger's logs released in 2009 under FOIA? Why are several pages from that document missing? Why are the logs for United 175 completely missing in the so called "Printout of ARINC logs" made public in December 2011?
>
> The answers to the above questions will probably shed light one day to what really happened to United 175. Understanding what really happened to United 175 is the key to understand what really happened on 9/11.

Something that the FBI does not seem to seek.

Plane Swaps?

ACARS messages prove that two of the four 9/11 aircraft were more than 300 miles from the spot where they supposedly crashed. Since this is impossible, could there be another explanation than the existence of two other planes?

This is the conclusion that the Woody Box blog comes to in an article called *Two "Flight 175" taking off from Boston Logan: CONFIRMED*. It begins as follows:

> My personal 9/11 researcher "career" started with the detection of a duplicated "Flight 11" at Boston Logan Airport: one departing from Terminal B, Gate 32, at 7:45, the other one from Terminal B, Gate 26, somewhat later because the departure was delayed.[296]

There are no further explanations. Let us make note of the following passage on p. 405 of *The Timeline Terror*:

> According to the 9/11 Commission, NEADS is contacted by Boston flight control. A controller says, "I just had a report that American 11 is still in the air, and it's on its way towards_ heading towards Washington....That was another_it was evidently another aircraft that hit the tower. That's the latest report we have....I'm going to try to confirm an ID for you, but I would assume he's somewhere over, uh, either New Jersey or somewhere further south." The NEADS official asks, "He_American 11 is a hijack?... And he's heading into Washington?" The Boston controller answers yes both times and adds, "This could be a third aircraft." Somehow Boston is told by FAA headquarters that Flight 11 is still airborne, but

296. *Two "Flight 175" taking off from Boston Logan: CONFIRMED*, Woody Box, December 30, 2008, http://911woodybox.blogspot.com/2008/12/two-flight-175-taking-off-from-boston.html.

the commission hasn't been able to find where this mistaken information came from.

If there had been two Flight 11s, it could not. The author of the Woody Box continues his analysis as follows:

> As opposed to that, the gate departure of United Airlines 175 is indisputable: **7:58 a.m.**, which is also confirmed by the database of the Bureau of Transportation Statistics (BTS).[297]
> However, the BTS database reveals a strange discrepancy regarding the "wheels-off time" of Flight 175 — i.e. the moment when the plane lifted off from the runway. The BTS notes a wheels-off time of **8:23**, which differs distinctly from the "official" wheels-off time, which is **8:14**.
> This **8:14** take-off is confirmed by the ATC/pilot radio transcript and various radar data. So what about the **8:23**? How was this datum being generated?
> The wheels-off time of is triggered automatically by a mechanical switcher when the plane loses contact to the ground. The data are sent automatically to the airline via ACARS, and the airline forwards them to the BTS on a regular base. So apparently no human failure is possible. The fact that the gate departure 7:58 coincides with the official story suggests that the data are valid.
> Being familiar with the duplication of Flight 11 at Logan Airport as well as the duplication of Delta 1989 at Cleveland Hopkins Airport, I arrived at the inevitable conclusion that this was another case of a duplicated plane — i.e. a "Flight 175" taking off at **8:14 and** another "Flight 175" taking off at **8:23**.

However, the author humbly points out that he was unable to find an independent analysis corroborating his work. He subsequently

---

297. This link to the BTS is no longer available.

added information found in *Touching History* confirming take-off at 8:23 of a "flight 175"[298]: a US Airways pilot on flight 6805, Steven Miller, stated he was taxiing behind Flight 175 on the runway and saw it flying away. After a quick check on the BTS database which revealed that USA 6805 was wheels-off at 8:28, the author explains that:

> Miller explicitly describes that he waited 3 minutes before getting takeoff clearance; adding a little bit for the time span between takeoff clearance and actual wheels-off, Flight 175 must have lifted off the runway around **8:23-8:24**. It is out of the question that Miller observed a plane that took off at **8:14**. Did Miller maybe see a different United plane? Very unlikely. Searching the BTS database for other United Boeing 767's delivers no results for the relevant time. There is a very slim possibility that a non-domestic United Boeing 767 took off just then, because the BTS database lists only domestic flights. However, Miller himself says it was Flight 175; so either he overheard the flight number when taxiing out, or, as someone who was frequently flying from Logan (as he says) he was familiar with the wide-body planes departing at that time.

If there had been two Flight 175s, the pilot's observation could not be a mistake. One of them would inevitably have been military, since airliners are subject to transponder and ACARS rules and cannot go undetected. On the subject, there is a testimony taken from the Pilots For 911 Truth forum, posted on January 19, 2012:

> I know from a USAF veteran who just happened to see it with his own eyes, that there were suspicious goings-on happening at Binhampton, NY, in the early hours of 11 September. He felt certain he accidentally witnessed some sort of military

---

298. *Touching History*, Lynn Spencer, Free Press, 2008, p. 58.

operation with a Boeing aircraft behaving very strangely there, and it is entirely possible that it was a drone Boeing. Speculation on his part and mine, but it did happen.[299]

Then the message adds:

> [...] the radar records show 11 and 175 crossing paths over the old Stewart AFB in Newburgh, NY. That would be an ideal place to swap planes if it were going to be done.

AA77 Swapped Too?

In several Pilots For 911 Truth articles this hypothesis is explored. Here follows a few excerpts:

> Flight Data Recorder Expert Dennis Cimino has confirmed that the data being provided through the Freedom of Information Act (FOIA) by the National Transportation Safety Board (NTSB) is missing crucial information, which according to Dennis, should be present and link the data to a specific aircraft and fleet. The NTSB provided three sets of data through the FOIA for what they claim is from American 77, N644AA. A csv file, an animation reconstruction and a raw data file. Rob Balsamo of Pilots For 9/11 Truth along with numerous other aviation experts, including trained Aircraft Accident Investigators have analyzed these files and determined they do not support an impact with the Pentagon. The data also exceeds the design limitations and capabilities of a standard 757 by a wide margin. This is based on data, precedent and numerous verified experts, including those who have actual flight time in the aircraft reportedly used for the 9/11 attacks.[300]

299. http://pilotsfor911truth.org/forum/lofiversion/index.php?t21761.html.
300. *Flight Data Expert Confirmation: No Evidence Linking FDR Data to American 77–FDR Data Exceeds Capabilities Of A 757, Does Not Support Impact With Pentagon*, http://pilotsfor911truth.org/Dennis-Cimino-AA77-FDR.html.

Dennis Cimino, whose expertise is beyond any doubt, then delivers technical explanations proving that the data given by the NTSB cannot be linked to Flight 77 specifically. Therefore, this data can stem from any plane, which is an impossibility in civil aviation. Consequently:

> So, if the data is not from N644AA, does not support an impact at the Pentagon, and in fact exceeds the capabilities and performance of a standard 757, what caused the damage at the Pentagon? That is exactly what Pilots For 9/11 Truth are trying figure out and the reason there needs to be a new and truly independent investigation. Some wish to ignore this data, some without expertise attempt to analyze it while attempting to say, "nothing to see here folks, move along."

Pilots For 911 Truth refused to "move along" and pursued its analysis:

> 02/28/11 — (PilotsFor911Truth.org) It has been reported that American Airlines Flight 77 departed Washington Dulles International Airport at approximately 08:20 AM on the morning of September 11, 2001 allegedly from Terminal Concourse D Gate 26 (1). However, the Flight Data Recorder positional data provided by the National Transportation Safety Board tells a very different story.[301]

The article continues with a comparison of images and graphs showing that the plane did not leave from Gate 26, south-west. Instead it would have departed from another gate, further north. The analysis concludes:

---

301. *Aircraft Departure Gate Positional Data Conflicts With Government Story,* http://pilotsfor911truth.org/aa77-gate-position.html

Once again the data being offered by government agencies do not support their theories.

Is this a possible aircraft swap before they even left the ground? Pilots For 9/11 Truth discover evidence of possible airborne aircraft swaps as well in their latest release "9/11: Intercepted". In almost 10 years since the attacks of 9/11, there hasn't been any evidence offered thus far which supports the government version of events, nor evidence linking their data to their reported allegations.

If the plane swap did occur, it could have been made before takeoff or when Flight 77 disappeared from civil radars. Indeed, the 9/11 Commission reported that its transponder had been turned off at 8:56 and even primary radars (p. 9)—which allow tracking despite an inactive transponder—lost it. It is a strange hijacking tactic, because turning off a transponder acts as a warning signal which can entail interception by the USAF or worse. In this case the risk involved in an interception was even higher, as the plane immediately disappeared from all screens since Ohio ATC only had secondary radars. Muslim terrorist apprentice pilots were likely unaware of this. Nevertheless, as a result, the plane disappeared from **civil** radars.

According to the Commission, at 9:32, controllers in Washington spotted a high-speed aircraft heading towards the White House on their primary radars. Here it could not have been Flight 77. As air traffic controller Danielle O'Brien stated, the characteristics of this unknown plane did not fit those of a commercial airliner. The *9/11 Report* omitted this information:

> The speed, the maneuverability, the way that he turned, we all thought in the radar room, all of us experienced air traffic controllers, that that was a military plane.[302]

---

302. *Pentagate*, pp. 96-97.

Thus, as Thierry Meyssan wrote:

> These civilian sources thus confirmed that an unidentified aircraft, flying at high speed and with great maneuverability was headed for Washington. But on the other hand, they didn't say that it was a Boeing 157-200 and still less that it belonged to the American Airlines company. On the contrary, they thought it was a military aircraft.
>
> It was therefore neither the civilian air traffic controllers nor the airline company that identified this vehicle as being flight AA77. The identification of the aircraft was made entirely by the army. Once again, the sole source is military.[303]

Besides, it was only later that afternoon when

> the connection with American Airlines Flight 77 was suggested to the press by anonymous military personnel. This "information" then spread among the media like a rumor. Only the *Los Angeles Times* specified its sources: it reported that officials "speaking under the condition of anonymity" explained to journalists that the Pentagon had been hit by Flight 77.[304]

Why request anonymity in such a situation? Was it Flight 77 or not? Was there any risk in saying so? Why did it take so long to announce that this was the plane? As noted by the Woody Box, top American Airlines management initially thought that Flight 77 had crashed into the South Tower. He adds:

> There were also rumors going around that a plane crashed near the Ohio-Kentucky border (as confirmed in Richard

---

303. *Pentagate*, p. 97.
304. *Pentagate*, p. 96.

Clarke's *Against all Enemies*), which is exactly the area where Flight 77 vanished (take a look at the Flight Explorer animation in the transcript link).[305]

And he concluded:

> Flight 77 crashed or landed somewhere near the Ohio-Kentucky border, and the plane that was detected by the Dulles controllers was not Flight 77. [...]
> Whatever happened to Flight 77, its official flight path after 8:56 is pure speculation, and the evidence suggests that it did not fly back to Washington at all.

Of course, we are in no position to check all these facts. Only the FBI can. The double plane hypothesis would still solve many anomalies and inconsistencies, including the impossible ACARS messages. For those who think it beyond belief, for technical or moral reasons, we recommend reading the Northwoods Operation of 1962.[306]

However, this scenario opens a can of worms. Now the Muslim apprentice pilots can no longer be the culprits of 9/11. But, before pointing fingers, the most crucial question is what happened to the passengers and crew members.

Neither Flight 11 Nor Flight 77?

It would seem that two Flight UA175s took off from Boston a few minutes apart. What of the other planes?

It was, for example, discovered in 2003 by independent

---

305. *Where was Flight 77 after 8:56?*, The Woody Box, August 21, 2007.
306. For example, in *9/11 The Big Lie*, p. 198 onwards. There is also a Wikipedia page.

investigator Gerard Holmgren and ascertained by the present author that according to the BTS[307] database of the US Department of Transportation (DoT), flight AA11 was not scheduled to fly at all on 11 September 2001 but were scheduled to fly on the preceding and subsequent days.[(46)] After Holmgren's discovery was publicized on the internet, the DoT hastily added the records for flight AA11 on the 9/11, fraudulently manipulating official records to correspond with the official account on the crime. If flight AA11 did not take off on 9/11, it would mean that passengers, crew (and possibly hijackers) boarded other, unidentified, aircraft.[308]

This passage refers to *Evidence that Flights AA11 and AA77 Did Not Exist on September 11, 2001*, by Peter Meyer.[309] He begins by reminding that the BTS

is reported to log every domestic flight scheduled from a US airport and conducted by a carrier accounting for more than 1% of domestic air traffic, and the database is required to include all scheduled flights, whether actually completed or not, unless the flight is cancelled more than seven days prior to the departure date.

The author then explains the charts and looks at flights on September 10 and 11:

The results (where, for a tail number, "UNKNOW" is the BTS entry presumably meaning "unknown") are:

---

307. BTS: Bureau of Transportation Statistics.
308. *There is no evidence that Muslims hijacked planes on 9/11*, Elias Davidsson, 10/1/2008, p. 7. Note 46: Gerard Holmgren, 'Evidence that Flights AA11 and AA77 Did Not Exist on September 11, 2001', 13 November 2003. Available at http://www.serendipity.li/wot/aa_flts/aa_flts.htm.
309. http://serendipity.li/wot/aa_flts/aa_flts.htm.

Date	Flight no.	Destination	Scheduled departure	Tail no.	Actual departure
Sept. 10	UA93	San Francisco	8:00	N570UA	7:57
Sept. 11	UA93	San Francisco	8:00	N591UA	8:01
Sept. 10	UA175	Los Angeles	8:00	N618UA	7:59
Sept. 11	UA175	Los Angeles	8:00	N612UA	7:58
Sept. 10	AA11	Los Angeles	7:45	N321AA	7:41
Sept. 11	AA11	Los Angeles	7:45	UNKNOW	0:00
Sept. 10	AA77	Los Angeles	8:10	N632AA	8:09
Sept. 11	AA77	Los Angeles	8:10	UNKNOW	0:00

So according to this information Flights AA11 and AA77 were scheduled on September 11. One might wonder, however, why there are no tail numbers for the scheduled flights. If planes were assigned to those flights then the tail numbers would be known in advance of September 11, but the tail numbers are listed as "unknown." And if those flights actually occurred, why are the entries for actual departure time given as "0:00"?

But, more importantly, this information is not what was originally given on the BTS website. Up until sometime in 2004 queries to the BTS database returned different information. The results of these queries were reported by Gerard Holmgren in November 2003 and later updated here. (*This page has now, January 2012, disappeared.*)

Peter Meyer then provides the links where the data had been backed up before its disappearance from the BTS website. Here follows a summary of the initial information:

Date	Flight no.	Destination	Scheduled departure	Tail no.	Actual departure
Sept. 11	UA93	San Francisco	8:00	N591UA	8:01
Sept. 11	UA175	Los Angeles	8:00	N612UA	7:58
Sept. 11	AA11	No record exists			
Sept. 11	AA77	No record exists			

Thus for September 11, 2001, and for Flights UA93 and UA175, the destination, tail number and departure time are the same as that given above. But for Flights AA11 and AA77 the situation is totally different—these flights are not scheduled at all. The implication is that Flights AA11 and AA77 did not exist on September 11, 2001.

The results are so unbelievable that we also analyzed the charts with detailed statistics for the departure of each plane.

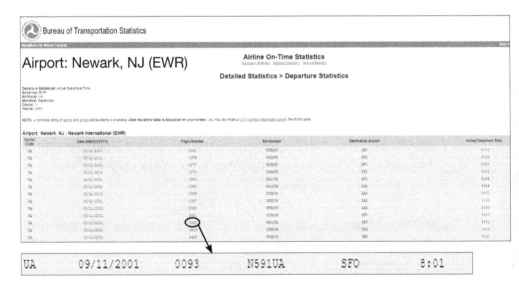

We see that a Flight UA93 registered N591UA really took off at 8:01 from Newark to San Francisco.

Likewise, Flight UA175 registered N612UA left Boston for Los Angeles at 7:58:

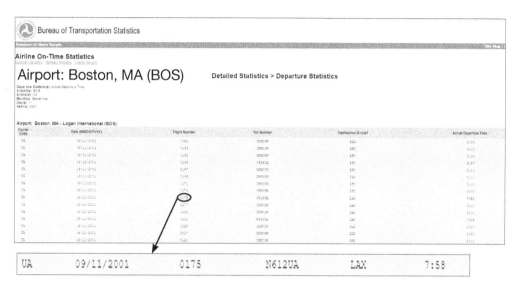

We now focus on the two American Airlines flights:

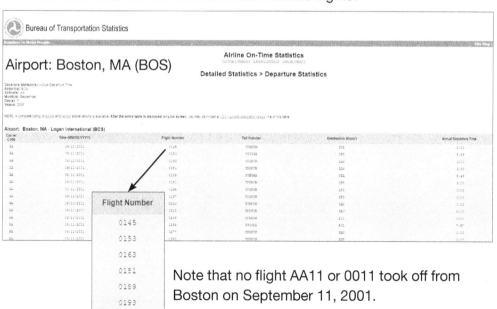

Note that no flight AA11 or 0011 took off from Boston on September 11, 2001.

And for Flight 77:

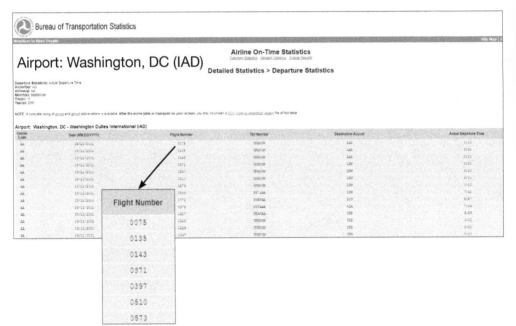

Same conclusion: no flight AA77 or 0077 left Washington Dulles on the morning of September 11.

How can this be? Naturally, al-Qaeda could not have tampered with the data. And even if they could, it would have been of no interest. Could the BTS have made two impossibly coincidental errors? Could the article or backed-up data have been faked? To what end? The criminal charges would be dire. Furthermore, flight diversion records confirm these first observations:

Flight number	Diversion records exists in:	
	original BTS records	current BTS records
UA93	Yes	No
UA175	Yes	No
AA11	No	No
AA77	No	No

Thus the records for the diversion (alleged hijacking) of UA93 and UA175 were removed from the BTS database. This was presumably done to disguise the fact that although, in the original database, there were records for the diversion of UA93 and UA175, there were none for the diversion of AA11 and AA77.

The reason why there were no records for the diversion of AA11 and AA77 is that these flights did not exist.

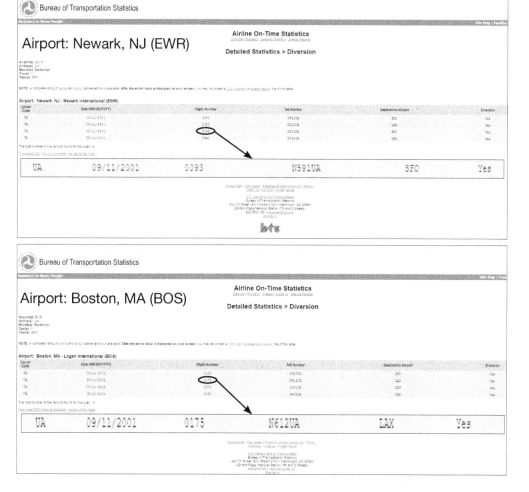

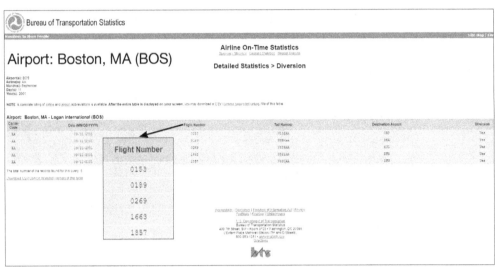

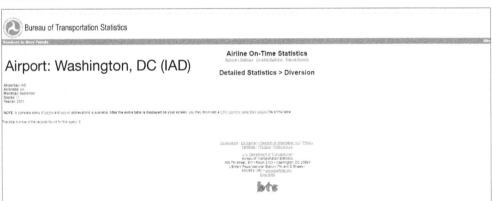

Should the information be true, we will let readers draw their own conclusions, especially since the article offers more information:

Further evidence for this can be found by considering the Airline On-Time Statistics.

Peter Meyer cites the BTS website pages where the data can be found. He uses Flight UA93 as an example, narrowing the search between September 10 to 11:

A page appears which gives data for UA 93 on September 10th, but above this is a note:

On September 11, 2001, American Airlines Flight #11 and #77 and United Airlines #93 and #175 were hijacked by terrorists. Therefore, these flights are not included in the on-time summary statistics.

But this note was added sometime after November 2003. Before that the same query (but for September 11, 2001, only) produced the page shown here. [hyperlink]

In the original BTS database similar queries returned the following pages for UA93, AA11 and AA77. Thus the summary on-time statistics (over any specified time period) for the four flight numbers differ in the current version of the BTS database from the version which existed until sometime in 2004 in this respect: In the original version that summary included data for UA93 and UA175 on September 11, 2001, whereas data on AA11 and AA77 is explicitly stated to be non-existent. But in the current version, data for all four flights on September 11, 2001, is excluded. This change was made presumably to disguise the fact that Flights AA11 and AA77 did not exist on September 11, 2001.

(Since the charts are fundamentally similar to those mentioned above, we consider their addition redundant. However, they can be viewed using the links within the article.)

Peter Meyer concludes:

> Consequently the official story, put out by the Bush Administration on September 11, 2001, and maintained without change for over four years now [eighteen years], is false. Arab hijackers could not have hijacked Flights AA11 and AA77, and crashed them into WTC1 and the Pentagon, because those flights did not exist. All the talk of Arab hijackers armed with

box cutters and intent on the destruction of the Twin Towers must have been a concoction, a hoax, designed to cover up what really happened on 9/11, and, of course, to conceal the identity of the real perpetrators of this atrocity, in which about 3,000 people were killed.

His conclusion starts with three questions:

Of course, if Flights AA11 and AA77 never existed then there are questions to be answered.

1. What of the Naudet video, which is claimed to show Flight AA11 crashing into the North Tower?

This video is the principal evidence put forward that a hijacked passenger jet was flown into WTC1. But there is good evidence that Jules Naudet's *9/11* film was staged, in other words, that the Naudet brothers had advance knowledge of the attack on WTC1, and positioned themselves in just the right spot to capture the explosion on video. If this is so then this in itself refutes the official story, since the alleged Arab hijackers or their leader are very unlikely to have informed the Naudet brothers of their plans. And if it is so then we can have no trust in the video, since it was made in order to provide "evidence" to support the official story, and it is not implausible that Jules captured only the explosion on tape, with the fuzzy flying object being added back in the video lab, before the tape was released to the media 24 hours later (though it can also be argued that he captured one or more real objects flying into WTC1, just not a Boeing 767).

The Naudet brothers "advanced knowledge" remains a theory. It is possible that they had originally been there for their documentary and filmed instinctively since the camera was on. Note that the FBI confiscated the Naudet brothers' tapes before returning them, meaning that there could have been tampering. Were this the case, the Bureau's complicity would be irrefutable.

Meyer's second question concerns the eyewitnesses who claimed to have seen AA77 fly into the Pentagon. He briefly responds to his own question:

> There are several reasons why these reports are not admissible as evidence […].

They are convincing but do not concern our study about the FBI. Here is the third question:

> 3. What about the passengers on Flights AA11 and AA77? Obviously, if these flights did not exist then there were no passengers (or crew members) on them. So what about the passenger lists for these flights? We must draw the obvious conclusion: These passenger lists were fake. They were supplied to CNN, *Newsweek*, etc., by the perpetrators as "evidence" to support the official story. Some of these passengers were probably fictitious (with "memorial websites" later set up by the perps), but there were also real people whose names were included on these lists (e.g., Barbara Olson) so one has to ask which of them are still alive (and where) and what happened to those who are not.

To whom should we ask these questions? The FBI?

Flawless Identifications?

While this chapter shows that Flight 77 could not have crashed into the Pentagon, government narrative supporters release their ultimate counter-argument: the identification of the passengers, crew members and hijackers' bodies proves it beyond a doubt.

How certain is this information? Here is what David Griffin had to say:

> The reason for uncertainty began when the FBI immediately took complete control of the Pentagon crash site. Dr. Marcella Fierro, the chief medical examiner of Virginia, pointed out that it was her office's responsibility to carry out the autopsies. But the FBI insisted that the autopsies be carried out by the Armed Forces Institute of pathology at Dover Air Force Base. Also, when the bodies arrived at the Dover Institute, they were brought by the Army and accompanied by the FBI.[180] Therefore, although the remains of reportedly 189 bodies were evidently delivered to the Dover Institute with word that they had all come from the Pentagon, there is no independent evidence that all of them were actually brought from that site.
>
> The victims of the Pentagon attack were taken to a temporary morgue in the Pentagon's north parking lot loading dock. They were then trucked to Davison Army Airfield at Fort Belvoir, then flown by helicopter to Dover. "FBI agents rode in the trucks, participated in the escort, and accompanied the remains during the flight to preserve the chain of custody." [...]
>
> But remains from the pentagon site could have been mixed at Davison with remains of bodies from elsewhere.[310]

A morbid theory that has to be posited when knowing that Flight 77 could not physically have crashed into the Pentagon. It once more raises the agonizing question: what happened to the passengers and crew members?

---

310. *9/11 10 Years Later*, pp. 234-235.

A Message in a Bottle... in a Stomach?

It is with a mysterious anecdote that we end the chapter. Several media outlets relayed that a message hidden in a passenger's stomach was found during autopsies of Pentagon victims. The person swallowed it before dying. The discovery was only revealed in 2015, when bestselling author Brad Meltzer visited the Dover Port Mortuary while conducting research for his novel, *The Escape Artist*. He asked a mortician if there was any way a person could hide a message inside their body before dying. Here is the answer:

> "[...] if you're on a plane that's going down, if you handwrite a note and eat it, the human stomach has enough liquids to protect the note from burning" in the fire that erupts when the plane crashes, Meltzer will later recall. The mortician will then tell Meltzer that this "really happened" on 9/11.
>
> [...] He will say that after the remains of the victims of the Pentagon attack were brought to Dover Port Mortuary, "When the morticians worked on one of the bodies, they found a note inside." Apparently, according to the mortician, "as the plane was going down, one of the victims on Flight 77 actually ate a note, which was found by a Dover mortician." He will call the passenger's note the "ultimate message in a bottle." He will refuse to tell Meltzer what it said, though. Meltzer will assume that the note must have been written by someone in the military, since, he will comment, "Who else would know that the liquid in your belly could preserve a piece of paper?" (*Washington Post*, 3/4/2018).[311]

Here is how the article ends:

> The FBI has a liaison at the mortuary while the remains are

311. Source: HistoryCommons.org, *Between September 13 and September 29, 2001): Morticians Discover a Note in the Stomach of a Passenger from Flight 77.*

being identified, in case evidence is uncovered during the identification process. (Pentagram, 11/30/2001; Rossow, 2003, pp. 95; Condon-Rall, 2011, pp. 75). The secret note is presumably passed on to this liaison after being recovered from the victim's stomach.

Did it reveal the true perpetrators of 9/11? Whatever the note said, the FBI seems to have done its utmost to keep the contents hidden. For all eternity?

To conclude this final chapter, it seems that anomalies and contradictions were piling up in the government's version of the conspiracy. The FBI's priority should therefore have been to investigate and clear up the countless grey areas making this narrative unlikely, or even impossible.

Unless the Bureau had another agenda, meaning that it had not "failed and failed and failed and failed and failed"[312], but rather "lied and lied and lied and lied and lied."

---

312. Quote attributed to Thomas H. Kean, Chair of the 9/11 Commission, in *9/11 Synthetic Terror Made in USA*, Webster Griffin Tarpley, Progressive Press, 2005, pp. 21-22.

Conclusion

Lies That Destroy a Nation

The Government Version of the Conspiracy

Our main goal throughout the book was to provide an overview of the FBI's real contribution to 9/11, without being exhaustive in terms of facts, events, anomalies and inconsistencies—which would be impossible in a single written work. Therefore, we recommend reading the research on which our study was based, along with other authors who doubt the government version of the conspiracy. Paul Craig Roberts, Assistant Secretary of the Treasury for Economic Policy in the Reagan Administration, provided a recap:

> Let's take a minute to re-acquaint ourselves with the official explanation, which is not regarded as a conspiracy theory despite the fact that it comprises an amazing conspiracy. The official truth is that a handful of young Muslim Arabs who could not fly airplanes, mainly Saudi Arabians who came neither from Iraq nor from Afghanistan, outwitted not only the CIA and the FBI, but also all 16 US intelligence agencies and all intelligence agencies of US allies [...].
>
> In addition to outwitting every intelligence agency of the United States and its allies, the handful of young Saudi Arabians outwitted the National Security Council, the State Department, NORAD, airport security four times in the same hour on the same morning, air traffic control, caused the US Air Force to be unable to launch interceptor aircraft, and caused three well-built steel-structured buildings, including one not hit by an airplane, to fail suddenly in a few seconds as a result of limited structural damage and small, short-lived, low-temperature fires that burned on a few floors.

The Saudi terrorists were even able to confound the laws of physics and cause WTC building seven to collapse at free fall speed for several seconds, a physical impossibility in the absence of explosives used in controlled demolition.

The story that the government and the media have told us amounts to a gigantic conspiracy, really a script for a James Bond film. Yet, anyone who doubts this improbable conspiracy theory is defined into irrelevance by the obedient media.[313]

Thierry Meyssan suffered the same fate the moment after *9/11 The Big Lie* was published in French, rather unsurprisingly after reading his conclusion to the first part:

Given the unprecedented means of investigation at its disposal, the FBI should have devoted itself to elucidating each of the contradictions that we have raised. It should have given priority to studying the message sent by the attackers to the Secret Service in order to identify them. It should have established what really happened at the Pentagon. It should have tracked down the insider financial dealers. It should have discovered the source of the messages sent to Odigo warning occupants of the World Trade Center two hours before the attacks took place. Etc.

Instead, as we have seen, far from conducting a criminal investigation, the FBI has applied itself to making clues disappear and silencing testimony. It has supported the version of a foreign attack and tried to strengthen its credibility by divulging an improvised list of the hijackers and fabricating false evidence [...].

This manipulative operation was orchestrated by its director,

---

313. Paul Craig Roberts, *9/11and the Orwellan Redefinition of "Conspiracy Theory"*, June 19, 2011, www.globalresearch.ca/9-11-and-the-orwellian-redefinition-of-con-spiracy-theory/25339.

Robert Mueller III, a key Bush appointee who coincidently took office the week before September 11.

Was this pseudo-investigation conducted to prepare for an equitable trial, or was it rather meant to hide from view domestic American culpability and justify the military operations to follow?[314]

A Suspicious Special Counsel?

Thousands of construction specialists were not duped by the government version either. Three towers as strong as the WTC could not have collapsed with such a speed after being hit by two planes. A property developer was interviewed in the evening of September 11, 2001, by Channel 9, New York:

> Channel 9: There is a great deal of questions about whether or not the damage and the ultimate destruction of the buildings was caused by the airplanes, by architectural defect or possibly by bombs, or after-shocks. Do you have any thoughts on that?
>
> Developer: It wasn't architectural defect. The World Trade Center was always known as a very, very strong building. Don't forget that it took a big bomb in the basement (in 1993). Now the basement is the most vulnerable place, because that is your foundation and it withstood that. And I got to see that area about 3 or 4 days after it took place, because one of my structural engineers actually took me for a tour because he did the building. And I said "I can't believe it." The building was standing solid and half of the columns were blown out. This was an unbelievably powerful building if you know anything about structure. It was one of the first buildings that was built from the outside. The steel, the reason the WTC had such

314. *9/11 The Big Lie*, pp. 59-60.

narrow windows is that in between all the windows you had steel on the outside of the building. That's why when I first looked at it you had big, heavy I-beams. When I first looked at it I couldn't believe it because there was a hole in the steel. And this was steel that was... you remember the width of the windows of the World Trade Center, folks, I think that you know, if you were ever up there, they were quite narrow and in between was this heavy steel. I said: How could a plane, even a 767 or 747 or whatever it might have been, how could it possibly go through the steel? I happen to think that they had not only a plane, but they had bombs that exploded almost simultaneously. Because I just can't imagine anything being able to go through that wall. Most buildings are built with the steel on the inside around the elevator shafts. This one was built from the outside which is the strongest structure you can have. And it was almost just like a can of soup.

Channel 9: You know... we were looking at pictures all morning long of that plane coming into Building #2. And when you see that approach the far side, then all of a sudden within another millisecond the explosion pops out the other side.

Developer: Right. I just think that there was a plane with more than just fuel.

Those who know this interview recognized the property developer as no other than Donald J. Trump, who would become the 45th President of the United States. He knew from the onset that the government narrative faced many inconsistencies, maybe even that it was a lie since he also saw what happened in Washington. Being a construction and real estate tycoon, he knows that a Boeing 757 with a wingspan of 38 m could not disappear into a 5 to 6-meter-wide window without damaging the rest of the building.

Now, he is under investigation for any possible links and/or coordination with the Russian government during his presidential campaign, which could lead to his impeachment. The Special Counsel in charge of this investigation is Robert S. Mueller, former Director of the FBI and one of the key men in Operation 9/11. He is the one who, a year after the attacks and despite all the proof collected from the Bureau's agents, still dared to claim:

> To this day we have found no one in the United States except the actual hijackers who knew of the plot.[315]

Did he even care to look? And what exactly was the Kean-Hamilton 9/11 Commission searching for, keeping in mind that President Bush and his Administration only created it after being forced by public opinion? Why? What did they have to hide? David Griffin can all but conclude that:

> The Commission also evidently sought, implicitly, to give a thorough defense of the White House, the Justice Department, the FBI, and the CIA by thoroughly omitting, or explaining away, any reports that could be used to suggest complicity on their parts.[316]

Physics for Dummies

Time and again, conclusions drawn by the FBI and 9/11 Commission defied the most basic laws of physics:

- three strong steel buildings collapsed in free-fall while only two had been hit by planes, in their upper levels and not even near the base.
- phone calls were miraculously made from cell phones at altitudes impossible for planes that are not equipped with on board systems;

315. *The New Pearl Harbor*, p. 69.
316. *The 9/11 Commission Report – Omissions and Distortions*, p. 13.

– suicide-bombers were declared dead when they were alive and well in their countries;

– a 38-meter-wide Boeing disappeared, engines and all, into a six-meter hole in the ground floor without major damage to the Pentagon facade and the lawn remaining intact (ambitious scientists, especially those seeking to succeed at any cost, claim that the aircraft's wings folded upon making contact with the building—since when do Boeings have foldable wings?);

– then this plane—a ghost since no camera in Washington could spot it and because it was unrecognized by air traffic controllers— "evaporated" or "gasified," as there was clearly nowhere near 58 tons of wreckage found in the Pentagon. Strangely enough, pieces of furniture and books next to the vanishing metal were almost intact;

– planes emitted signals from areas where they could not be according to the government, and continued to communicate after being destroyed;

– Flight 93 literally vanished into a small hole with nothing sticking out;

– the FBI was able to rebuild almost an entire airliner from practically nothing, and certainly not from the tons of metal that should have been at the Flight 77 crash site.

Had September 11 not been a horrific disaster that is still taking lives in Afghanistan and elsewhere, one would have thought it was a government practical joke. Lives will keep being wasted if we fail to act.

The FBI: A Culprits' Nest?

Too many inconsistencies and anomalies make it impossible for this extraordinary agency—among others—to blame this catastrophic failure on incompetence or misfortune, as they have been trying to make us believe for all these years. Therefore, opening a real investigation is necessary to at last expose 9/11 in its entirety, no matter the nationality or allegiance of the culprits and their accomplices, and even if some of them were within the FBI.

It should, for example, be determined who in the hierarchy blocked investigations—that could have avoided the attacks—by agents that had advanced knowledge of the date, methods, targets and perpetrators of the crime? Who threatened them with lawsuits if they went public with the information? Who gave the order allowing the bin Ladens and other Saudis to leave the country while civil aircraft were grounded? Who decided that the unprecedented insider trading was insignificant and deemed it useless to investigate disaster speculators? Who confiscated, lost, and maybe cut the most telling videos on events in Washington? Who ordered the claim, among others at the Moussaoui trial, that the Boeing 757 was almost complete in an FBI warehouse, whereas the military had declared in press conferences that only the two black boxes and a beacon had been uncovered? What pushed FBI agents to silence witnesses in New York, Pennsylvania, Florida and other areas? Who decided not to investigate the compelling ACARS messages that contradicted the government narrative of the conspiracy? These are only a sample of the questions that must be answered.

It is not too late, and essential, to search for and establish responsibility and complicity in 9/11. Then, an FBI-orchestrated cover-up should be looked at through its successive directors, namely Louis Joseph Free who resigned in June 2001, Thomas Joseph Pickard, director from June 25, 2001 until Robert Swan Mueller III's nomination in early September 2001, as well as their closest staff. Indeed, *The FBI, Accomplice of 9/11* concerns mainly its directors and managers, not the dedicated and exemplary field agents who sometimes valued their duty more than orders from above. Some even dared to break the silence and speak out against their superiors, knowing that it would ruin their careers and labeled them as whistleblowers.

FBI top brass are not the only targets of the investigation. To the list must be added John Ashcroft, George Tenet, George W. Bush, Dick Cheney, Ronald Rumsfeld, Paul Wolfowitz, the members of the 9/11 Commission, etc. Barack H. Obama and Hillary R. Clinton must also be looked at. Among others, they were key in escalating the Afghanistan war effort, "liquidated" the already dead Osama bin Laden and stirred up (civil) wars in Libya, Syria and elsewhere, including Ukraine. How can it be claimed that the American people gained anything from this when they lost so much?

Conspiracy Theories

Since 9/11 is a conspiracy theory with thousands of victims of which there is not yet the final draft, could it be linked to the *Russiagate* of 2016? Perhaps we should jump back a few years to put things into perspective.

On February 11 and 12, 2015, three mainstream media journalists died within 24 hours: Ned Colt (NBC) dropped dead of a stroke; Bob Simon (CBS) died in a car crash; David Carr collapsed in the newsroom of the *New York Times*. A fourth, Brian Williams, was suspended by NBC at the same time for six months. Thereafter, a report prepared by the Russian Foreign Intelligence Service (SVR) revealed that these top US newsmen had something in common explaining why one had been "effectively destroyed" and three of his colleagues killed: they were about to release evidence that 9/11 had been an "inside job" undertaken by their own government. President Vladimir Putin had allegedly made a source from the Russian archives available to them. Therefore, the Obama Administration may have silenced them for bearing the truth.

Without a copy of this report, neither its contents nor its existence can be determined. Regardless, on February 7, 2015, five days before the journalists' death, *Pravda* published an article titled *US Fears Promulgation of Russian Satellite Photos of 9/11 Tragedy*. The following paragraph provides an extract:

Russia is preparing to release evidence of the involvement of the U.S. government and special services in the September 11 attack. [...].

The published materials will be able to prove the evil intent of the government towards the people of the USA and successful manipulation of public opinion. The attack was planned by the American government, but was carried out by outsiders. Thus, the attack on America and the people of the United States looked like an act of aggression of international terrorism.[317]

Therefore, *Russiagate's* main goal would naturally have been to impeach Donald Trump, and if this failed, public hysteria would be fueled daily by anti-Russian media and influencers, discrediting any proof and documents Russia could make public.

In any case, the death of these three journalists may just have been an unfortunate coincidence, and perhaps they were not about to unveil anything. Otherwise, they would join the long list of 9/11 victims. On a passing note, after *Pentagate* was published in 2002 I saw a video in Dutch on YouTube showing that seventeen American citizens, whose testimonies contradicted the government version of the conspiracy, had died under "questionable" circumstances. Then again, it could just be the law of series, misfortune and coincidence working together, as has so often been the case in the history of the United States. What is certain is that al-Qaeda was not responsible for these deaths if they were not natural.

To be or not to be?

We cannot predict the future. However, if Robert Mueller's investigation brings Donald Trump on the road to impeachment, we can expect the latter to play a "Trump" card revealing the truth

---

317. *США боятся обнародования российских спутниковых фото трагедии 9/11*, *Pravda*, February 7, 2015.

behind 9/11 and its true culprits. And even if the impeachment fails, until when will he be able to keep the time-bomb ticking?

Leading up to this earth-shaking truth—and it will out—we wonder when the American people will at least wake up and realize what 9/11 and the War on Terror really are. When will they notice that the more it expands, the poorer they get, to the sole benefit of an intelligence and military body linked to banks and media that are constantly getting richer at their expense? Has the American people been this poor since the Great Depression, despite the government claiming the opposite? And what remains of the American Dream? Was it reduced to rubble along with the World Trade Center?

Only the American People can find the answers. Nobody else will save them and, as the verse goes, "God helps those who help themselves." The more time goes by, the more difficult it will be to get back up, especially since other world powers are progressing at a lightning pace. It is high time to rise up before it is too late.

If not, who will still believe in the self-proclaimed "exceptionality" of the American people so blessed by God?
Can America be great again?

Paris, January 13, 2019

Bibliography

9/11 The Big Lie, Thierry Meyssan, Carnot, 2002.

Pentagate, Thierry Meyssan, Carnot, 2002.

The War on Freedom: How and Why America Was Attacked, September 11, 2001, Ahmed Nafeez Mosaddeq, Joshua Tree, Calif.: Tree of Life Publications, 2002.

1000 Years for Revenge: International Terrorism and the FBI–the Untold Story, Peter Lance, Harper Collins, 2003.

Die CIA und der 11. September, Andreas von Bülow, Piper Verlag, 2003.

The Terror Timeline, Paul Thompson, ReganBooks, 2004.

The New Pearl Harbor, David Ray Griffin, Arris Books, 2004.

Crossing the Rubicon, Michael Ruppert, New Society Publishers, 2004.

Cover Up, Peter Lance, ReganBooks, 2004.

Against All Enemies: Inside America's War on Terror, Richard A. Clarke, New York: Free Press, 2004.

The 9/11 Commission Report – Omissions and Distortions, David Ray Griffin, Arris Books, 2005.

The 9/11 Commission Report, W.W. Norton & Company.

America's "War on Terrorism", Michel Chossudovsky, Global Research, 2005.

9/11 Synthetic Terror Made in Usa, Webster Griffin Tarpley, Progressive Press, 2005.

House of Bush House of Saud, Craig Unger, Gibson Square, 2007.

9/11 Ten Years Later, David Ray Griffin, Haus Publishing, 2011.

The Terror Factory: Inside the FBI's Manufactured War on Terrorism, Trevor Aaronson, Ig Publishing, 2013.

The 2001 Anthrax Deception: The Case For a Domestic Conspiracy, Graeme MacQueen, Clarity Press, 2014.

Table of Contents

9 781913 191009